MW01613613

LIFE-

stories from the harbor

New Life
Raymond, WA

GOOD CATCH PUBLISHING

Copyright © 2005 New Life , Raymond, WA. and Good Catch Publishing, Beaverton, OR.

All rights reserved. Written permission must be secured from the publisher to use or reproduce any part of this book, except for brief quotations in critical reviews or articles.

This book was written for the express purpose of conveying the love and mercy of Jesus Christ. The statements in this book are substantially true; however, names and minor details have been changed to protect people and situations from accusation or incrimination.

Published in Beaverton, Oregon, by Good Catch Publishing.
www.goodcatchpublishing.com
V1.2

Printed in the United States of America

TABLE OF CONTENTS

ACKNOWLEDGEMENTS

We offer heart felt thanks to all the people of New Life for their friendship and inspiration. Whether your personal story is in this book or not, it's your book. We love you and value every one of you. To each person who shared their story, we are honored and humbled to live with such people. We are proud to be your pastors.

We would like to give special thanks to Heather Milton, who was the project manager here at New Life. She worked diligently throughout her pregnancy carrying not only a child but this book project forward.

To Brianna Lindley we are so grateful, for her skill in consulting this project. Thank you, Bri, for producing a first class cover.

Peggy, thank you so much for the gift you have given this community! Your love, care and work are such a powerful gift. We deeply appreciate the talent you used to help us tell our story to our city. Your pen brought such life and fullness to each story. We love you and are so thankful that you were our writer.

Finally, thank you to Daren Lindley and Good Catch Publishing for bringing the entire concept to life. It would never have happened without you and your awesome team.

Sincerely,

Dwayne & Janna Deskins
Senior Pastors of New Life

Introduction

On the pages before you are true stories of real people just like you and I, living and loving through difficult events in their lives with real results. The remainder of their story is still being written.

CHAPTER 1

Diane's Story

"You're a liar!"

He slammed down the magazine he had been reading so hard it made me flinch! His words rang through the air like a shot! My body jerked with the impact!

"Dad!"

"You heard me! You're lying!" He stood up and pointed a finger at me, his rage written all over his face!

"No! I'm not! Dad, listen…" My palms were perspiring and anxiety seized me! I couldn't believe what was happening!

"Diane, how dare you say something like that about a member of our family!"

"Dad, honest! He took me into his room and…"

"That's enough! I'm telling you, that's enough! Don't you dare repeat that lie to anyone else! Do you hear me, young lady?" My mom butted in.

My mother and father, my source of love and security for 15 years of my life, turned there backs on me, strode out of the room and slammed the door behind him!

I stood there, motionless! My heart was pounding so hard I could hear it in my ears! I didn't know whether to cry, run, scream, or throw up! "He doesn't believe me!" I

Diane's Story

thought incredibly to myself!

Tears welled up in my eyes and slid down my cheeks. Through the blur somehow I managed to stumble out of the room and get outside. I walked aimlessly, anywhere to escape what had just happened! I was in shock!

I found myself in the backyard and flopped down on the cool, soothing grass behind some low-lying shrubs. I lay there, in a fetal position, my mind spinning frantically! "What am I going to do?" I thought as I sobbed!

It was true, of course. A member of the family had been molesting me since I was 5 years old. It had taken me 10 years to work up the courage to tell my father, and when I did a bomb went off in my face! I had expected understanding, nurturing and love. Instead, I was assaulted by his rejection, my security pulled out from beneath me like a rug!

I stayed curled up in the grass for a long time. It was dusk when I heard my mother calling out the back door that dinner was ready. Reluctantly I got up, straightened out my clothes, wiped at my face with my hands, and went into the house. I approached the dinner table, slowly, cautiously, trying not to call attention to myself. I slipped into the nearest chair, keeping my gaze down. I didn't want to see my father's face. But, try as might, I couldn't endure to sit at the same table with these people who would not believe me when I told them my most painful secret.

Excusing myself, I quietly got up and left the table. I went to my room.

That was how my relationship with my father was going to be for a long time. We avoided each other. It tore me up, because he and I had always been so close. I felt like my lifeline had been cut and I was cast adrift. I was so hurt that the idea of getting "even" with him started to grow in my mind. That's how I survived. "I'll find a way," I told myself.

My grandma had taken me to church growing up and I would see a few of my neighbors there, but ours was far from a "Christian" home. I knew about Jesus and the things He could do. I memorized some scripture, and could quote it with ease, but after this incident with my father my faith died. I gave up. I gave up one God and found another. Drinking, partying, guys, and sex. I knew I was on a

Diane's Story

path to hell, but I just didn't care.

I met Dirk when I was 17 years old. He had red hair and was wearing a plaid flannel shirt and a pair of stone-washed jeans. When he smiled he was all green eyes and white teeth. I was very attracted to him. He showered me with attention and gifts. I was starved for affection and attention, and I was flattered that he wanted to be with me.

Dirk came to my house one afternoon. We were sitting on the couch listening to CD's and Dirk had his arm around me when my father came home from work.

"What's *he* doing here?"

"Uh, hi, dad. This is Dirk!"

My father stood there, staring at both of us. "What have you been doing?"

"He's my boyfriend." I stammered.

Dirk stood up and said, "Hi, Mr. Anderson." He stuck his hand out to shake hands with my dad.

My father didn't make a move to reciprocate, and Dirk tried to inconspicuously put his hand down.

"Diane, I would like a word with you! In the kitchen! Now!"

LIFE— stories from the harbor

I got up off the couch and followed him into the kitchen. I felt like a little puppy that had just had an accident on the floor.

As soon as I got inside the kitchen, my father whirled around to look at me, his face contorted with anger! "I want him out of here! He's a piece of trash!"

"How can you say that? You don't even know him?" I flared.

"I'm going to give you 10 seconds to get him out of here, and I'm starting to count now!"

As I hurried out of the kitchen, I heard him say, "And don't ever bring him back here again!"

I walked into the living room, my face flaming with embarrassment. I was sure Dirk had heard us. "Come on. Let's get out of here!" We went outside.

"What's his problem anyway?"

"Nothing! He's always like that with me!"

"Maybe this will make you feel better," he said. He reached into the pocket of his jeans, pulled out a tiny black box and handed it to me.

"What is it?" I squealed.

"It's for you! Open it!"

Diane's Story

I carefully opened the lid. Inside there was a tiny gold ring knotted in the middle by two connecting hearts.

"It's lovely! Oh, thank you, Dirk!"

"It's a friendship ring. Put it on!" He smiled at me, as he watched me slip the ring on the fourth finger of my left hand. I dropped the box on the ground outside the house, and we took each other's hand and dreamily walked to his motorcycle.

I felt so lucky that Dirk wanted me. Nothing in the world could have convinced me to give him up. I was wondering to myself why my father had taken such an immediate dislike to Dirk, and then it struck me! "That's it! Dad hates Dirk! He doesn't want me near him! Wonderful! I finally have a chance to get even!"

Within a couple of months I discovered I was pregnant! That wasn't part of the plan! I was filled with anxiety and worried sick about telling my family! But I lost the baby in the third month. Not long after that I had my eighteenth birthday. Immediately after, Dirk and I decided to get married. I broke the news to my mom, but I never said a word to my father. I left that job up to her. To my utter amazement my mom gave us a nice wedding.

We were married in our church, and I wore a beautiful long white gown.

But my father would not "give me away." Instead, in a last-ditch effort to "rescue" me, offered me $10,000 NOT to marry him. I walked down the isle alone.

I was positively glowing! Nothing was going to spoil my happiness! I felt that I finally had love and security! I cried a lot that day, and just bubbled over with hope and joy!

Halfway through the reception, at the peak of my ecstasy, I felt a firm hand grab my arm in a painful grasp and jerk me back from a friend with whom I was speaking. Turning around, I saw my new husband with an unusual scowl across his face.

Pulling me into a corner he threw out his index finger which he proceeded to use to punctuate his points as he nearly yelled, though somewhat under his breath, "Let me tell you about the rules, bride!"

"What's the mater with you?" I said in shock.

"Shut up and listen, dirt bag!"

What's going on? Am I having hallucinations? Is this my husband?

Diane's Story

"Rule Number 1: You are not going to come first in my life, so forget that idea!

Rule Number 2: I will be out with my friends, male and female, most of the time! Don't even think about saying anything about it!"

God! God! I just got married! This is my husband! He promised to love me, honor me, protect me!

"Rule Number 3: If I'm not out with my friends, you belong to me to with as I see fit," he said with an undeniable tone of innuendo.

"Stop! Dirk, stop!" I sobbed.

I had a nearly impossible time enduring the rest of the reception with my friends and family, trying to believe that what had just happened was some sort of bad dream, a hallucination.

It was not, and my wedding night was no improvement. Rather, he showed me just what exactly he meant by those threats.

The next morning, when Dirk was in the shower, I frantically called my parents! My father answered the phone!

"Dad! Dad!" I cried.

LIFE— stories from the harbor

I blurted out the words before he even had a chance to say "hello."

"I want to get an annulment! I need help, dad!"

"Diane, I told you he was no good! You made your bed, and now you can lie in it!" Click.

He hung up! He hung up on me!

I quietly replaced the phone in its cradle. My intention to get revenge on my dad had backfired on me! My life was in ruins!

I started drinking to dull the pain in my heart. When I was 20 I discovered I was pregnant with our first child. The abuse continued throughout my pregnancy, and it was a miracle that I managed to carry the baby to term and deliver a healthy boy. *A miracle! Yes!* As soon as I had that thought my heart leaped and I knew that I had been protected by someone greater than myself. I cried out to Him! "Lord! Lord! I need you so much!" I fell to my knees! "Jesus, I know I have turned my back on you! I'm so sorry! Please help me!" A bit of scripture ran through my mind. *O Lord, I have come to you for protection; don't let me be put to shame. Rescue me, for you always do what is right (Psalm 31:1).*

Diane's Story

Four weeks after the birth of our son, my husband took off for four weeks! I had no idea where he was or if he was coming back. In my heart I prayed that he wouldn't come back, but I had no idea how the baby and I would survive without him. I couldn't go to my parents for any kind of help—not the way things were between my father and me. Besides, their marriage was in big trouble, and my mom had recently told me she was going to file for divorce.

My husband returned after his 4-week absence, and when our son was 5 months old I found I was pregnant again! Not only that, a lump had been found in my breast and my doctor told me I should probably abort the baby. "If this turns out to be cancer, we won't be able to treat it with chemo if you're pregnant."

"No! I won't do that!"

The tumor grew rapidly, and I had to have it surgically removed. I made the arrangements and told my husband I needed him to drive me to the hospital for the procedure.

"Too bad, bride. I gotta work. *Someone* around here has gotta work!"

"Dirk! This is serious! How am I going to get there?"

"Walk," he said as he slung his jacket over his shoulder and left the house. "It's party time," he told me in a sing-song voice. He gave me a wink and went out the door.

My mother took me, but had to drop me off so she could go on to work. I felt absolutely alone and abandoned. I knew no one in the world cared about me. Again I prayed. *O Lord, you are my rock of safety. Please help me; don't refuse to answer me. For if you are silent, I might as well give up and die. Listen to my prayer for mercy as I cry out to you for help, as I lift my hands toward your holy sanctuary (Psalm 28:1-2).* I believed that God had abandoned me too.

The surgery was a success, and the tumor was benign. I went into labor on New Year's Eve. This drove my husband into a rage!

"You can't be serious! It's New Year's Eve!"

"I can't control this!" I yelled back at him.

"Listen to me! It's party time!"

At that moment, I started bleeding heavily!

Diane's Story

"Dirk! My God, am I going to lose this baby? Please!

"Hang on, bride," he said quietly. "I'll get the car keys!"

I will never know what made him calm down and decide to take me. Our second son was born the next day. There was some blood in the baby's lungs when he was born so they kept him in the hospital for a couple of weeks.

I was caught off guard when we brought the baby home from the hospital. We had had some freezing weather. The pipes were broken, there wasn't any water, refrigerator, washer or dryer—it was a nightmare! I knew it was going to take both Dirk and I working together to handle this emergency.

Dirk took one look at the mess and said, "That's it! I'm outta here!" Without another word, he grabbed up the car keys and took off. I stood in the middle of the room holding a newborn in my arms and a toddler clinging to my leg.

We huddled around a cooking stove to keep warm. The next morning a friend stopped by to visit, saw what a mess we were in, and went to the store for groceries. I was determined that we would survive and get along without him. Between my mom and some friends we hung on. Unfortunately for me, he came home after a few weeks. I didn't have the nerve to call it quits. Somehow I felt I needed him! I even told myself I loved him! It was sick, and I knew it! I just didn't have the courage to leave him.

Apparently God was not answering my prayers, and things got steadily worse. Dirk's rages became more frequent and more violent. One day I was in the kitchen fixing lunch. Dirk came up behind me, grabbed me around the neck from behind and started dragging me backward! He dragged me into the living room where the children were playing! I saw them and my mothering instincts took over! I fought for my life, but to no avail! He grabbed me by the hair and began pulling it out! He threw me to the floor, kicked me in the back, and when I rolled over he stomped on my stomach! The kids were shrieking with terror as they watched their father beating up their mother! They hovered together on the couch, clutching each other for dear life! I managed to stagger up to my feet, but he grabbed my long hair again and threw me to the ground!

Diane's Story

My neck cracked loudly and I thought for sure it was broken!

Dirk left me lying there. He went outside and vented his rage on his motorcycle! He had a large piece of wood in his hands and he was banging up the bike, trying to trash it. I staggered into the bathroom, grabbed a washcloth, ran some cold water on it, and started to wash my face! My gaze lifted to the mirror and everything froze. I stared at my bruised and bloody face. I saw my scalp where hunks of hair had been yanked out.

Resolve built up inside me! There was no way I was going to let my kids grow up in this environment! I wasn't going to take it any more! I was afraid he would become abusive to the children!

I grabbed the kids and the car keys! When Dirk finally came back into the house, I calmly told him I was leaving.

"You chicken!" he shouted. "You're nothing but a dirt bag! You can't do anything!"

I watched him go into the kitchen, and soon I heard the pop of a beer can. I fled out the door, piled the kids into the car and drove off. I didn't realize at the time that I was pregnant with our third child.

I drove along the coast. I could see the broad, shimmering band of the Pacific Ocean stitched to the shoreline. Before me, the day was so clear, I could almost count the mountain ridges. Clouds were peering over the mountaintops, a fast-moving blanket of dark gray in advance of a storm. That night was the first of many that the children and I lived in the car.

I stuck it out. I was determined to make a go of it. I had three children and a lot of help. The divorce was in process, and both Dirk and I couldn't wait to get it over with. I managed to get a small apartment, and I was able to work a little bit. However, things got to the point where I was having difficulty just getting food for the kids. I was too proud to ask for help from DSHS. My back was against the wall, and I felt panicky and desperate. I got on my knees and cried out, "God, I need help! I know I have sinned and wandered so far away from you! But... I need food for my children!

Please help me!" I got up from my knees and wandered aimlessly through the apartment. I wondered if He would ever hear my prayers again.

Diane's Story

I heard a knock at the door. I opened it and my brother was standing there. His arms were full of grocery bags!

I cried with relief as I let him in! He told me he had been driving home when he felt a strong urge to go get groceries and drop them off at my place! Everything I needed was there! God had heard me! He answered me! I burst into tears!

"Randy! I prayed to God for help about 45 minutes ago, and He sent you!" He looked somewhat bewildered!

"That's awesome! It's a miracle!" He gave me a big hug, then teased, "If you don't stop crying, I'm gonna take them all back!"

He stayed for dinner. I was so humbled and grateful standing there cooking a small dinner for all of us. But I forgot to thank the Lord.

I wish I could say that I cleaned up my life right away after that, but I was so lonely I continued my habit of going to bars to hang out with people. I drifted from guy to guy. I couldn't stand to be alone.

I was beginning to feel convicted about my lifestyle. A little voice inside would speak to me, but I brushed it off. "No! Go away!" I wouldn't admit to myself that it was God trying to bring me back to Himself.

An amazing thing happened! The house where I was born and raised became available to me. It belonged to my dad, but he'd moved to another house with his new wife and this one was vacant. Some time back we had called a kind of truce, and we developed an "okay" relationship, at least superficially. He called me one day and told me we could move into the house. I did not bring any alcohol or drugs into that house. Something inside me just wouldn't let me do it. I still went to the bars and drank, but God was starting to show Himself to me in new ways.

One day I was driving home from the beach with the children, who were now 2, 4 and 6 years old. We found ourselves driving through a tremendous rainstorm! The water pounding on the top of the car sounded like a drum beat, and the wind was blowing so hard the rain blew in sheets sideways across the road. The car started sputtering!

"What's wrong! I wondered, a feeling of panic chewing at my insides. My gaze fell to the gas gauge. Empty! "Oh, Lord! Please don't make me walk in this

Diane's Story

storm with the children!" No sooner had I prayed these words, then I noticed the gas gauge slowly moving up from "empty" to "full!" The hair on the back of my neck stood up! I wondered if I was hallucinating! Could God really have answered my prayer that fast? I had just witnessed a miracle! I said a prayer of thanks, and from that moment on prayer became a part of my life. I started living my life differently, small changes at first, but soon big changes were being made.

I wanted to attend church. I had heard some good things about New Life, but somehow I just couldn't bring myself to go. I even drove around the church several different times and wondered what was going on inside, but I just didn't have the courage to take that step and go find out for myself. One day I mentioned this to a friend, and she said, "Hey! Come to church and find out!"

I tentatively, even fearfully, went to church one Sunday. Near the close of the service, I felt the Holy Spirit urging me to go to the front for prayer. I was trembling! I was in strange territory—a place where something supernatural had control. The pastor prayed, and I recall him saying, "God forgives you for getting a divorce. He's not angry with you. He loves you." I cried for three weeks! That's how long it took to purge myself! At the end of that time I felt as if the weight of the world had been lifted from my shoulders!

I wanted to be baptized as soon as possible! I spoke to the pastor about this, and he set it up. The entire week before my baptism I prayed and worked hard to surrender my whole life to God. Everything about my life that I had held inside I let go and gave to Him. I told God there were four very important changes I wanted to make in my life right away: I wanted to stop swearing, I wanted a hunger to read the Bible, I wanted to be healed from all the pain I had suffered and I wanted to be free from fear—the terror that kept me from sleeping at night. "Lord, I've surrendered my life completely to you. Please help me!" *I will praise you, Lord, for you have rescued me. You refused to let my enemies triumph over me. O Lord my God, I cried out to you for help, and you restored my health. You brought me up from the grave. O Lord, you kept me from falling into the pit of death (Psalm 30:1-3).*

I put the children down for their naps and started

Diane's Story

picking up the house. From time to time a vision danced through my mind. It was like a flashback to a painful moment in my life. I sat down in an armchair, laid my head back, and closed my eyes. The visions continued. I didn't understand what was happening, and I was afraid!

As each scene presented itself to me, I felt like I was physically floating to a level just above it! I had a number of these visions, and with each one I floated higher and higher! Within moments I realized that I was finally high above all of it! All the pain, abuse, accusations, obscenities screamed at me—it was all gone! It was an awesome experience! "Thank you, Jesus!"

I developed an enormous need to read my Bible! I read over half of it in just two weeks! I took it everywhere I went. One day I noticed that I wasn't swearing—and hadn't been for a while. It just went away! I had also slept with ease the last couple weeks! As soon as my head hit the pillow, I was gone! What an enormous change! I used to sit up at night with a spotlight and a gun, afraid that Dirk would sneak around and try to kill me!

I brought charges of domestic violence against my ex-husband. I was very nervous thinking about going to court to face him. There really wasn't any evidence because I had never called the police to report him. I believed he would never be convicted, and I was afraid of retaliation. The night before I was to appear, the Lord put a scripture in my heart from Matthew 10:26. *Therefore do not fear them. For there is nothing covered that will not be revealed, and nothing hidden that will not be known.* It brought me such peace and comfort. The judge found Dirk guilty and sentenced him to jail time and community service.

Doors opened up for me so I could attend college! It wasn't long before I was telling my class-mates all about what God had done for me! About this time I found myself in financial difficulty, with no job and no money. I cried out to the Lord! He didn't waste any time answering. The next morning I answered a knock at my door. Someone had delivered a food basket with 30 sacks of groceries! Everything I could possibly need was in there, including light bulbs, toothpaste, and band aids! During the next few weeks the Lord's provision overwhelmed me! Someone paid my house rent, and someone else my attorneys fees. I

Diane's Story

found that daycare for my kids had been paid. I received a phone call and was offered a job! Finances were provided so I could finish school!

I reflected on the fact that my father had never acknowledged that I had been molested. We had never talked about it. I thought we had mended our fences and through the years grew to have a reasonably normal relationship. I came home from church one day, and my mind replayed things that he and I had done together, places we had gone, games we had played, all the fun things we had done. Then I started to remember all of the bad things. "Lord, my dad and I are okay now. What's going on?"

In my heart I knew I was going to have to talk to him about the resentment that I still held in my heart toward him because he never stood up for me or protected me. I began praying to God to let me know the right timing for this. While I was praying, my phone rang. It was my father!

"Hello?" I asked.

There was a slight pause, and then I heard, "Diane? Is that you?"

"Dad?" My heart softened immediately.

I plunged right in! "Dad, you know what happened to me and we've never talked about it. You called me a liar and told me to shut up about it! I was deeply hurt, and I felt anger and resentment toward you all these years. I'm sorry for feeling this way, and I want you to forgive me. I love you!"

"No! I'm the one who's sorry! This has been eating me up for years! I didn't know how to act toward you or what to do! I know life would have been different if I had only done the right thing! I should have gotten help for you, and I'm so sorry, Diane! I love you too, honey!"

Healing at last! The weight of years of pain and rejection evaporated!

The Lord has been able to use me in so many different ways. I had the opportunity to counsel a person who was on the brink of suicide. I was able to do that because I experienced it myself. I'm involved in Life Group, Prayer Group, and Women's Bible Study. I frequently get the opportunity to share what He has done in my life and tell my story. For the first time I feel content. God has been so good to me! I am truly free at last!

Diane's Story

I will praise the Lord at all times. I will constantly speak his praises. I will boast only in the Lord; let all who are discouraged take heart. Come, let us tell of the Lord's greatness; let us exalt his name together (Psalm 34:1-3).

CHAPTER

2

Patrick's Story

"Look at that chick!" my buddy yelled. We were pretty loaded. For no particular reason, he slid his upper body up and out the passenger window. With his legs braced against the console, he was free to use both hands to make an obscene gesture toward the girl. "Hey, $#*@, you want some of this?" We laughed and continued around the block. Flopping back in the seat and laughing hysterically, he yelled, "Lets go back!"

Again he yelled, "You *&$#@," taunting the young girl and her apparent boyfriend, whose arms were covered from shoulder to palm with tattoos. This time they yelled back, matching our obscenities and raising us one. This was great. We had to go back and show that we were louder and more obnoxious.

As we rounded the corner our eyes searched the crowd of people wearing various gang colors, as we yelled and laughed. The couple seemed to have disappeared. We now started deriding them, laughing at their apparent inability to take our chiding. Suddenly a big, black Cadillac squealed its tires and pulled in immediately behind us. Its headlights flashed and several sets of arms were raised out the windows giving us "the bird."

Patrick's Story

Our laughter immediately chilled as the car revved its engine, racing up on our tail and then breaking at the last minute. These guys looked pretty tough and we weren't interested in getting shot. I yelled, "We're getting out of here!"

"No kidding," my previously loud-mouthed friend said.

Moments ago I had felt invincible in my mom's Jeep Cherokee. Now I wished I was in something that cornered a little better as I broke free into an open lane and raced forward. Our pursuers weren't even mildly fazed. Their engine roared as we came to a red stoplight. One of them got out of the car brandishing an aluminum baseball bat. Just then, the light turned green and I slammed the throttle to the floor. Racing to the next intersection, I saw that it was a one-way street headed left. I turned right!

Surely this will cool them. My adrenalin really surged when I saw the big Cadillac roar around the corner. Cars heading toward us swerved, flashed their lights and honked their horns, but they were the least of my concerns. The car continued chasing us.

"Come on, Pat," my friend half pleaded, half demanded, "lose this guy!"

I swore, "What do you think I'm trying to do, you idiot?" I ran off a long string of cursing as I vowed what I was going to do to those guys if we met, but beneath the façade, I was scared like never before. We led the traffic as we headed toward Burnside Street with the Cadillac immediately on our tail. The speedometer needle rotated to 70 miles per hour, then hit eighty as we swerved and careened through the streets of Portland. As I approached an intersection, I thought I'd fake a left turn and go for a right. When I swerved to the left, then back to the right, the Cadillac didn't do anything but barrel on ahead, connecting with my right, rear passenger door, pushing and rotating the car 90 degrees to the right. I hit the throttle again now running for my life. Our car now pointed toward the river and First Street where our chase had begun. When we got to First Street we headed south, the Cadillac still on our tail. As we approached Madison Street the river was on our left. The light was red and traffic was flowing into downtown Portland from the Hawthorne Bridge. Without hesitation I plunged into the traffic, somehow, miraculously, avoiding a

Patrick's Story

collision while passing through both lanes.

With Madison Street diminishing in my rearview mirror my friends looked back, but the Cadillac seemed to be waylaid. We had escaped. The car was eerily silent as we drove on. A real awareness permeated the car, that somehow we had narrowly escaped a brutal end. We felt the breath of death breathing down our collars and it chilled us all.

I had no purpose in my life. I was at the bottom of the bottom. From the moment I was born in Eugene, Oregon, I was nothing but trouble for myself as well as my parents. In the third grade I was diagnosed with Attention Deficit Disorder, or ADD, and we spent a lot of time going to various counselors. Both of my parents had been educated in the drug and alcohol field, and they did a lot of research while trying to figure out what would help me.

The doctors tried many different medications on me, and I had a different reaction to every one of them. I was up and down and all around the place, just so hyper! My parents never knew what to expect of me, and I didn't know what to expect from myself.

LIFE— stories from the harbor

From kindergarten through fourth grade, I was constantly in trouble. I attended a Christian school, and I got spanked a lot. In fourth grade, my parents moved me to a public school where things just got worse. I didn't understand things. I was rebellious and upset because I just wanted to be normal like the other kids. My home life was chaotic.

"Patrick? What are you doing?" my mom called to me.

I didn't answer her. I was running frantically around my room, turning things upside down, trashing things.

It was the same at school. On the school bus, I went wild.

"Patrick, sit down and behave yourself!" The driver was beside himself.

I never listened. Finally I got kicked off the bus.

"Mrs. Walton?" The school principal had called my mom. "I'm afraid we are going to have to suspend Patrick. He is just uncontrollable."

We lived in Eugene until seventh grade, and then moved to Washougal, Washington, a very small and close-

44

knit community. Everything took a spin for me. I was now the outsider. The other kids had been together ever since kindergarten and had established friendships. They really tormented me. They talked about me and cracked jokes about the "new kid." While I was getting off the bus, they knocked my hat off and my school bag out of my hands.

I thought I was a cool kid. After all, I was from the big city of Eugene. I knew how to snowboard and rollerblade. Washougal was totally different. The people were different. I found my group of friends among the skateboarders. They were a rough group, and most of them were one to two years ahead of me in school. But it didn't last, and I was kicked out of middle school in the seventh grade.

My parents were almost at their wits' end, so they decided to home-school me. They gave me the work to do and hoped I would do it. I was left on my own because they both left the house to go to work. After about two hours of study, I felt I had done enough and it was time to take off. I did whatever I wanted to do.

"Well, since I'm home alone, let's learn to

smoke," I told myself.

I started running with a bunch of kids who were hard-core meth users, until I was in the ninth grade. I am sure it was by the grace of God that I never tried the stuff. But I was running crazy. I spent a lot of time trying to fit in with this group of kids.

In the summer we went to Eugene for a short visit, and I visited with my old friends and neighbors. What a shock! I felt like I had entered the drug capital of the world.

"Hey, Patrick! Want to eat some acid?"

"Come on, Patrick. Try some mushrooms!"

I experimented with LSD and had a horrible trip. It was just a nightmare. All I can remember is crying and laughing, crying and laughing. We stayed up all night.

When we returned to Washougal, my parents threw up their hands with home-schooling and sent me to an alternative school. If you weren't making it in regular school, the alternative school was a place to go so they could try to salvage you, keep you from dropping out and help you get your diploma or GED. I couldn't have cared less. I was busy running around with friends. We went to Portland to attend concerts and small clubs. By this time, I was smoking a lot of pot and doing some drinking. I was on the brink of being kicked out of school again. The Washougal school district stepped in and set up a meeting with my parents, the Superintendent of Schools and me. Then something incredible happened.

"There's a special school in Portland called Serendipity," the Superintendent told my parents. "It will cost us about $5,000 a year to send Patrick there, but we believe he has some potential and we don't want to lose him. We will make that investment in him for one year. We will bus him from Washougal to Portland. Let's see if we can make this work."

I wondered to myself, "Why did they pick me to do this?"

I am sure my parents were wondering where things had gone wrong. Ours was a Christian home. My mom was a women's ministry director at a large church, and both my parents were actively involved in church. My sister was an incredible entrepreneur and very successful. But there was really something different about me. I didn't have a clue what it was and, apparently, no one else did either. I guess all of us were thinking that I was the "wild hair" in the family.

The school was crazy. I spent my time drawing pot leaves on my school papers. Others threw chairs at the teachers and stabbed their friends. There were padded, soundproof rooms where they would put you so you could hit, kick, scream and freak out. It was so bad that some of the kids even urinated and defecated in that room. Many of them were hard-core gang members from Portland. We even had 16-year-old drug pushers in the class.

The only good thing about that school for me was an incredible teacher named Jeff Richmond. He was brilliant. He was young, rode his bike to work and played Frisbee golf. He was so cool! He had a degree from some huge college in Boston. He had a wonderful way of teaching, and for the first time in my life, learning became fun. He taught a class on music. He would crack jokes about some of the songs, but he was never demeaning. He had an incredible way of meeting you on your own level. I remember a slogan he had hung on the wall in his room: "You are a bunch of dopeless hope fiends!"

Other people were thinking, "You are a bunch of

Patrick's Story

hopeless dope fiends!" His slogan was a great statement. It was Jeff's influence that got me to start thinking about going to the University of Oregon.

In eighth grade they told me I was pushing my limit there. They called a conference, and my parents and the Washougal Superintendent of Schools attended.

"Patrick, this is it. You are at the bottom of the bottom here. You have to make a choice because something drastic is going to happen."

One day I was walking through the park in Washougal. I was wearing my big, baggy pants, and had weed in my pocket. The wind had picked up and the trees seemed restless, stirring uneasily. The morning air was chilly and the earlier pale sunlight had faded as the sky clouded over with the threat of rain. As I walked along, a strange feeling started to overtake me. I reached into my pocket and my fingers sifted through the weed, as I tried to get my mind off whatever was reaching out to me. Suddenly I stopped. There was this vivid moment—it was just crystal clear. I stood there motionless. In the clarity of that moment, I saw exactly what was happening. I was trembling, and I felt very, very weak.

"What am I doing? I have to change!"

I took the weed out of my pocket, walked to the public restroom and flushed it down the toilet.

I ran home. My folks were there, and I said, "I want to change."

My parents took me shopping and I changed my wardrobe completely. No more "Mr. Cool." I chose more conservative clothing.

Next, I cut off old friends and made new ones. I stayed sober, and I didn't party.

I completed ninth grade and my folks and I got all dressed up for graduation. At the ceremonies they gave me an award. It was called the "Bob Award." The name of the man who founded the school was named Bob. The award was for the student who had made the most positive changes during the year. Out of 500 students they gave it to me!

My parents took pictures of me holding the "Bob Award" plaque. Everyone, including me, thought it was just amazing. I felt proud of myself, which was a feeling I was not accustomed to.

When I look back on that chapter of my life, I real-

Patrick's Story

ize that God had parted the curtain for me and gave me a look at what life could be like. It was a spiritual moment, and, at the time I made all the changes in my life, I didn't realize how badly I would backslide.

At the end of ninth grade, I was enrolled again in a public school in Washougal. This time it was very hard for me. It was so different.

I was walking down the hall, feeling weird, like I had some kind of stigma. I was edgy. Things were very quiet. I could hear them whispering.

"Look! It's him!"

"He's back!"

"Oh, my gosh! Is it really him?"

They remembered me from seventh grade, and what they remembered most was how crazy I had been.

After awhile, I began to fit in. I had a new circle of friends. They were the "popular" kids at school. My whole mentality about partying changed. My group didn't party through the week, but we couldn't wait for Friday and Saturday nights. That's when we would hang out and get stoned.

In eleventh and twelfth grades, I did a lot of group

partying. We went to downtown Portland to the underage clubs on Friday nights. We danced and met girls. I was getting more and more used to group partying and drugs.

I got a job at a car wash. One of many jobs I would lose in my life. As it would turn out, I would get fired from eight different jobs between ages 15 to 20. I was always calling in and asking for time off. The longest I held a job was three months. But I needed money so I could party. I met a really cool guy at the car wash. I thought he was neat, and I looked up to him. He was an "old school" break dancer. He was into the Rave scene, and he introduced me to it. The funny thing about the Rave scene is that people thought the kids were crazy and mixed up, but there were athletes, preps, varsity lettermen and jocks, all stoned and wearing crazy outfits. Hip Hop stuff! It didn't seem weird to me because I had been doing the group thing. I got very involved, and started eating ecstasy. Before long I got fired from the car wash. I had fallen asleep on the job.

When I was a junior in school, my parents wanted me to start thinking about going to college, a Christian college. There was a possibility I could go on a soccer scholarship. We tried a few colleges, and I played some soccer with the guys, but I wasn't motivated for the college deal and didn't do well. As I approached the end of my senior year, I became aware that my friends were beginning to look at colleges, and the day came when they took off. They went all over the place to go to college. They had a vision and goals. I was left behind with the unmotivated.

I enrolled at Clark Community College in Vancouver. Now I had my "old friends" back in my life. The ones who "weren't going very far." Just before enrolling at Clark, I had made an observation about myself and my drinking. No matter how much I drank, it was never enough. When my friends and I drank, I always had to have more. I wasn't satisfied with a couple of beers like they were. I always wanted to get drunk. I knew I was different, but I didn't know why. There was an edge about me.

Clark was an entirely new lifestyle to me. A whole new life of partying and getting loaded. None of us had parents around. We all had our own apartments, dorms, etc., and no one was watching over us. Such freedom! I wasn't interested at all in school. I was just going through the motions. My interest was in getting loaded and getting high. I ran with kids who were hard-core weed users, even some hard-core marijuana dealers. I often got stoned with them.

As time went on, my parents really became unhappy and discouraged with me. "You need to get yourself together. You're 20 years old and you can't hold a job. You need to figure something out."

I managed to get a job at the airport working for Avis, checking in rental cars. I figured out a way to work the system and ended up extorting money from the company. One day I was working my scam on a guy, and he turned out to be an Avis Corporate employee. I told him, "Hey, I'll help you out. Give me $20 and I'll check you in and mark the gas tank as full." Normally it cost $50 to fill up, but no one kept any records. I could make $20 or $30 off the customers and put it in my pocket. A week later they called me into the office. I felt a little weak and shaky walking over there. "What am I doing here?"

I sat down. "Have you been trying to get money out of the company? Are you taking money from anyone?"

"No! Not at all!" I lied.

Patrick's Story

"That's really funny because we've got the story. You did this to one of our Corporate staff members. Do you want to 'fess up?"

I squirmed in the chair, and felt a knot of fear in my stomach. "Well, I might have said..." Suddenly it all came out. They had me.

Before I left the airport that day, I had another job lined up with Huntleigh. I pushed wheelchairs and checked baggage. I had to take a urine test. Since it took about a month for the results to come back, they let me work in the meantime. I guess I wasn't too surprised when it came back dirty and I got fired, but I was very discouraged.

I thought, "There's a good way to cure the blues." I called some of my friends and we arranged to meet at a Rave in Seattle on Saturday night. Five of us decided to leave on Friday morning, and we all piled into an old Lincoln that belonged to one of them. We had a bunch of weed and a radar detector. It was pouring down rain and the windshield wipers didn't work. We drove about 90 miles per hour and we were smoking like crazy. The inside of the car was cloudy with smoke.

LIFE— stories from the harbor

We all got high.

When we got to Seattle it was about 9:00 p.m., and we stayed up partying almost the rest of the night. We ended up parked beside a Fred Meyer store and we slept in the car. Saturday morning I took my fake ID, the one I had used many times in clubs, and I went into a convenience store and bought three 24-packs of Budweiser. We decided to party until we met our friends later that night. We drove around and decided to park under a bridge by Safeco. We were well on our way to getting drunk when we met up with the other guys at 5:00 p.m. All of us continued to drink. We were trying to get high before we went to the Rave.

Around 9:00 p.m. we entered the building where the Rave was being held. It was a huge, multi-level monster, and there were about 17,000 kids partying inside. I ate two hits of ecstasy right away. We had been inside about 20 minutes when I became separated from my friends. I was suddenly overcome with a powerful feeling of loneliness. I will never forget it. I just stood there, rooted to the floor, and tried to take in the immensity of the evil scene.

It was dark in there, an ugly, thick darkness. You couldn't tell what people were doing, and it seemed to me

Patrick's Story

like the dead were walking around. Kids were sick and throwing up. It was the epitome of hell. I immediately felt a huge conviction. Something in me said, "You've got to get out of here!" but I brushed it off. I knew a life without Jesus was a life headed for destruction, but I put the thought out of my mind with another hit of ecstasy. The next thing I knew I was done. I was fried out. We had been partying from 5:00 p.m. Saturday until noon Sunday. We walked out of there on a bright Sunday at noon. I was disgusted with myself.

One of my friends drove the car, and I slept. I slept all the way to Washougal. When I got home, I slept the rest of the day. My dad asked me questions about the Rave and drugs. My parents knew something was up. I couldn't even answer them coherently.

By the time Monday rolled around, I felt like I was a little kid again as I said to my father, "Dad, I'm going back to bed. Will you come with me?" As I lay there we started to talk. I got very "real" with my father. I told him I was into ecstasy, that I must be crazy, and I knew I had to change. I told him about the Rave. He listened and talked to me. Then my dad shared something with me. He told me my grandfather had died from alcoholism, his mom had been a heavy drinker, one of his brothers also died of alcoholism, and another brother was an alcoholic. My dad also told me he was a recovering alcoholic. I had always known there was something different about me, and I never had a clue what it was, other than I had a propensity for drinking. Now I knew the alcohol genes were running rampant in the family.

"Dad, doesn't grandma have an extra room at her house? I need somewhere I can just go and stay. Somewhere I can get away for a bit."

"Yes, Patrick, I think she does."

We called her and she said I could come. She was living in Raymond. I heard later that when she hung up the phone she just freaked out. She told grandpa, "There's no way we can take Patrick into our house." She was 67 and grandpa was 75. They knew my past and didn't think they could handle this.

I went up there on a Friday. It was late September, and I thought, "I'll go work in the woods. Cut lumber. Be a man." The only stipulation my grandparents gave me about coming up to stay was that I had to go to church. I thought,

Patrick's Story

"I can handle that."

My grandparents had told their church that I was coming. "Make him feel welcome. He's our grandson."

Saturday I didn't do much. I was just hanging around the house. Sunday we got up and went to church. When we got home, I went to sleep. I was sleeping upstairs when my grandparents left to go to evening church. They didn't want to wake me. Something jolted me awake, and I woke up and sat up simultaneously.

"Church! I have to go to church! I have to be there!" I got up and ran down to the church. God brought me to church on Sunday, October 8, 2000. I listened in suspense as Jamie Joiner preached about the very thing my life lacked. I was captivated.

I sat on the edge of my seat, just rapt with attention. I had never been a part of anything like this in my life.

There was a heaviness in the air. I found it a little difficult to breathe.

My eyes were riveted on the piano player, who had started to weep. Within seconds, he got up from the keyboard and went over to another member seated on the platform, touched him on the shoulder, and *he* started crying.

"What's going on?" I wondered.

I felt something very powerful gradually start to work its way through my body. It was a gripping feeling that started to take over my heart, my thoughts.

The piano player had gone over to the pastor, and when *he* started crying, my palms started to perspire.

From the pastor, the man migrated over to the microphone, bowed his head and wept. I found myself holding my breath.

As he gained some control over himself, his voice rang out with the words, "There are some people who are here for the wrong reason."

I felt a stab at my heart. I felt immediately convicted. I had decked myself out in Abercrombie to come to church with my grandparents. I was a visitor at their church, and I wanted to impress people. It had nothing to do with God and everything to do with me. I felt prideful and stuck up. When we left home I had felt really cool, but I looked inside myself when he said those words, and I believed, without any doubt, that his words were directed toward me.

The man continued, "Whoever you are, if you will come right now, God will soften your heart. If you don't come, it will take you time in the Word and prayer to get back to *this* place."

Grandma stood up quietly and moved into the aisle. Intuitively, I knew she was moving aside so I could get out. There was something supernatural in the air, and it just picked me up out of my seat and put me into the aisle.

I slowly walked to the altar at the front of the church. My legs felt shaky and a ball of emotion started to knot up inside me.

When I reached the altar, I fell to my knees and I just broke. I cried with great sobs, gulping for air, and just poured myself out. It was a divine moment as I shed my old life at the foot of the cross. I heard the Holy Spirit saying things to me as I cried. The voice caressed me. "I will never leave you or forsake you. I will be with you forever."

"Yes, oh yes, Jesus!" I sobbed.

"I will be your partner, Patrick. It's going to be

me and you."

I felt surrounded with tremendous love and security. As my heart was rent before God, I groaned loudly, "Oh, Jesus!"

I was saved! My heart was full to the point of bursting.

Later, my grandparents told me of how my dad had been at a very similar place in life when he got saved at the same age. He was also 20 years old like I was. It was the same time of the year too, October! Grandma and grandpa weren't my real grandparents. They were a terrific couple that had been in the ministry for 50 years. When my dad was saved, they were rehabilitating hippies.

After my experience at the altar, my heart was just on fire. I was spirit destitute. I was in church every night of the week and twice on Sundays. I started reading the Word, but it was difficult for me. I wasn't a big reader. I would climb up on the kitchen counter while grandma was cooking and she helped me with the Word. I would feel so good. Then my parents got me a New Living translation. Without that, I don't think I could have read the Bible. The New Living translation brought life to the Word, just unlocked it.

Patrick's Story

I filled journal after journal with all my thoughts, various sermons, and even some revelations that came to me. I had all these writings. "What are they all for, Lord?" I asked. He didn't answer me right away, so I waited patiently on the Lord.

I went to a Valentine's Day service in Aberdeen with a good friend of mine. There were about 150 kids at the church. A young lady, part of the college ministry, asked me if I would share what happened in my life. "No problem." I shared, and afterward the pastor got up.

He said, "I believe the Holy Spirit wants to speak to my heart. Can we just take a minute to pray?" Quiet settled over us like a gentle blanket as we bowed our heads and prayed. I heard him say, "I have a word for Patrick. Patrick, you are on a roller coaster. It's at the top and it's just about to cut loose. It's going to be incredible. I need to pray for you. Will you come up?"

"Yes! Sure!"

He laid hands on me. The Lord powerfully touched me. The pastor began praying over me. As he prayed, I knew that I was called to preach the same good news that had so recently changed my own life. He said,

"Patrick, you have been pulled up out of the fire. It hasn't been of your strength, but rather God's. He has called you to preach the gospel. I don't know how that will look, but he has called you to preach."

It all began to make sense to me. Why I had all my writings, why I had such a burning in my heart, why I knew the minute I heard Pastor Jamie Joiner preaching in grandma's church that I *would love* to do that. I had been accumulating messages for the church. They had been hidden in my heart, just like God's Word.

I became a servant in the church. I started out doing all the maintenance work like weeding, mowing the yard and organizing clean-up days. Then I did the tape ministry and became an usher. I began to spend a lot of time with the pastor. I rode around with him. I wanted to serve him. In January 2003, he called me and said, "Patrick, I have a task for you. I want you to start a youth ministry for me." I wasn't sure that God had called me to that, but I told the pastor I would serve him any way I could.

Late one night, right before I went to sleep, I heard the Holy Spirit say, "Don't think it's strange that I have called you into youth ministry." The hair stood up on the

Patrick's Story

back of my neck and I just tingled all over.

I saturated myself in prayer, and read the Bible like never before. I decided not to date during this time. This was particularly difficult because I had just met Jennifer. She was so special. She was just so much more than anyone I ever thought I would meet, let alone date. But I had to tell her "no" about dating at that time. The Holy Spirit spoke to me in my heart, and told me she and I would get married someday. I prayed over her and watched her while she dated others. When the time was right God let me know, and Jennifer and I went out to dinner and have been together ever since. We were married in August 2005.

The Holy Spirit has put a lot of dreams in my heart for preaching at crusades, and preaching in front of great multitudes. When I quit McDonald's to serve the Lord, they begged me to stay. What a turnaround!

I will bless the Lord who guides me; even at night my heart instructs me. I know the Lord is always with me. I will not be shaken, for he is right beside me (Psalm 16:7-8).

CHAPTER

3

Sally's Story

"Do you know God? Do you know Christ? Do you know that you have eternal life?"

My last ride had just dropped me off. Sauntering down the sidewalk by the park, my bulky, beige sweater slung carelessly over my shoulder, those words grabbed my attention. "That's kind of cool," I thought, as I strolled into the park, getting closer to the group of hippies gathered there. The leader was standing on a wooden crate preaching at the top of his lungs.

"Believers can walk in the light of Christ and have fellowship with him!"

"I like that." I had never heard anything like it. Sitting down on one of the benches close to them, I continued to listen. I glanced to the right of the bench where a bunch of wild sunflowers were swaying in the breeze. Hues of yellow, gold and brown shimmered softly among the trees. I gazed at the awesome beauties, and reached out to pick just one. My eyes beheld the wonderful gold as it reflected the morning sun.

"Have you ever heard about Jesus?"

His voice startled me. Turning my head sharply, I saw a tall, young man with long, dark hair. He wore   tat-

68

tered jeans, a white tee shirt with "Jesus Lives!" emblazoned across the front, and a red scarf around his neck. A tender expression tugged at the corners of his mouth as he smiled at me.

"I asked if you have ever heard about Jesus." Specks of light sparkled in his brown eyes.

"No, I don't think so." I paused for a second. "Well, I think I have heard that name before, but I don't know anything about him."

He put out his right hand, palm up, and gestured to the spot beside me on the bench. "May I sit down?"

"Sure." I scooted over to make more room for him.

He sat down and started to talk to me about Jesus Christ. The things he said to me were very intriguing, and I was hanging on every word.

He paused, gazing at me thoughtfully. "You're not ready now," he said softly.

What a surprise! I wasn't expecting to hear him say that.

He went on, "When you *are* ready, get a Bible and read the book of John."

Smiling at me, he got up and made his way back to the group.

Something very important in my young life had just happened, but I wasn't sure exactly what it was.

I got up, tucked the sunflower in the hip pocket of my jeans, and walked around the perimeter of the group, eyes roving among the crowd, listening to their conversations. Many of them had books in their hands, and I supposed they were Bibles. The name "Jesus" was mentioned a lot, and I found myself wishing that I could be part of a group like that. It was a kind of family, and I didn't have one.

A young man came up behind me and started walking along beside me, matching his gait to mine.

"Are you on the road?" he asked.

"Am I wearing a sign or something?" I asked sharply.

We continued walking, with me half listening to him and the group at the same time.

He was undaunted. "My name's Justin. I'm hitchhiking to California. Where are you headed?"

"Nowhere special. I'm Susan." I softened the tone

of my voice.

"Want to come along with me?"

I put my arm out to stop him, and we came to a halt. I stood there and stared at him for a couple of seconds. Poking out from under his red knit cap were wisps of ginger-colored hair. He had small, mild blue eyes, pale brows, and a long, deeply creased face. It looked as though he hadn't shaved for days.

"Sure," I replied impulsively. "Why not!"

We were on our way to Anaheim. Just like that! That was my life. Drugs, hitchhiking and living moment to moment.

In Anaheim we went to a crash pad. Justin had found out about it from a friend of his. There were some other people in the house, and we all shared whatever we had.

Emptiness felt like a weight inside me. It was as if I was disconnected from people. I was continually searching for "my place" in the world. One night I dropped some acid. It never occurred to me that I might not be able to handle it. I knew I could take whatever amount I wanted and come back from the "trip." Until this evening. The room started spinning violently, my vision blurred, and I saw all kinds of hideous faces parading before me in gaudy hues of red, yellow and green. It seemed as if I was plunging downward into the depths of hell, flames licking at my body, and I screamed and tried to claw my way out. Total darkness enveloped me, and I found myself in a vacuum, swirling around and around. Thoughts were running rampant through my mind: "I have no purpose, no meaning to my life. I have no connection to anyone or anything." Realizing I couldn't separate the effects of the drug from reality, I screamed out, "God, if you are real, you better show up because I might not make it back!" *O Lord, hear me as I pray; pay attention to my groaning (Psalm 5:1).*

The next thing I knew I was out of it, a Bible clutched in my hands. I had stolen the Bible from a library while we were hitchhiking to Anaheim.

A couple of nights later another guy in the house came back from something he called a "Jesus Freak" rally. He had a fist full of pamphlets about Jesus. "Give them to me! What did they tell you?"

He sat down beside me and told me all about the

rally. The rest of that night, until dawn the next morning, I looked through the Bible. Significant things about Jesus were printed in bold, black letters. There was a page where it told you how to invite him into your heart. Reaching out to those words like a starving child, I did all the things it said to do. A soft, swirling warmth went through me. It seemed to lift me up higher and higher.

I was confused, not sure what to do next. Daylight found me back on the road, hitchhiking to Buena Park, California. After locating a crash pad in the area, I hitchhiked all over Los Angeles, witnessing for Jesus. "Isn't this what I'm supposed to do?" There was a big question in my mind. I felt like I wasn't going about it quite right.

Somewhat dejected, I wandered down the streets of Los Angeles, wondering what to do next. Then I remembered! Some friends had told me that in Palm Springs lots of hippies lived outside the town in the caves. Thumb out. I was on the road again.

The climb through the canyon up to the caves was exhausting. My thighs were burning, I was huffing and puffing, and my heart was rat-a-tat-tatting like machine gun fire. I could have sworn there was less oxygen in the air up there. Behind me, the clouds were peering over the mountaintops, a fast-moving blanket of dark gray in advance of a storm. I peered into my new home. It was dark as pitch in the cave, but it was a place to sleep and I put all my stuff in it.

It was near Easter, and I had hitchhiked down into Palm Springs to panhandle for food and money. There were quite a few mounted police all around the city that day. When I was ready to return to my cave, to my dismay, the police were at the entrance to the canyon.

"Hold it, miss! No one is allowed into the canyon."

"Why not? All my stuff is in there."

"Sorry, but we're not letting anyone in. Last year school kids on spring break trashed this area pretty bad, and we're making sure it doesn't happen again."

He was clean-shaven except for a line of whiskers he'd missed when his razor jumped over the cleft in his chin. His dark brows were fierce over dark, blue eyes.

I lowered my eyes, depression descending on me like a big, black cloud.

He paused to look at me. "You know, if you were

my daughter, I would want you to come home."

"If I were your daughter, I would like to go home, but that's not an option for me." I choked back a sob and blindly lurched down the street.

Wiping the tears from my eyes with the sleeve of my tee shirt, I soon found myself walking next to a guy who looked to have about the same misfortune as myself.

"I've seen you around town." He gulped a drink of soda.

"Yeah. Well, I live here."

He chuckled. "Yeah. My cave's the second one on the right."

We gazed at each other for a long moment, and then burst into laughter.

"C'mon. Let's sit down."

We found a bench on the sidewalk. "I guess we're both evicted," I said.

"Here. Have a Pepsi." He stared out at the street as he handed me the can. He took a drag on his cigarette, drawing deeply, clearly savoring the relief.

"Thanks." I popped the lid off the can. It was a steamy, hot day, and I appreciated the icy-cold, sweet, dark fluid as it slid down my throat.

His hair was dark, flecked with gray, and stringy. He glanced over, flashed me a smile. His eyes were a chocolate brown, and he had surprisingly white teeth. He was muscular, and his arms were knotted with veins and matted with thick, dark hair. A trickle of sweat angled down along his cheek, and he blotted the side of his face with the sleeve of his tee shirt.

He told me that he was going to Florida to do some political work. He invited me to go with him.

My quick assessment of him was that he was kind of crazy, so it absolutely amazed me to hear myself say, "Okay. I'll go with you. What's your name?"

As our trip progressed, Jake became more and more weird. I guessed he was on speed or something. His personality would change drastically, and he would become very unpredictable. We hitchhiked through New Mexico and Texas. When we got to Arkansas, he promptly ditched me. I had no ID, no clothing other than what was on my back. I was on the road again.

Man after man tried to assault me. "What am I doing out here? I don't even have any ID." At a truck stop a

Sally's Story

couple of truckers approached me. I hadn't slept in a couple of days, and my eyes were like burned out embers.

One of them asked, "What's wrong?"

The tears poured out of my eyes uncontrollably.

"My boyfriend ditched me. I need to get back to California."

"C'mon. We'll give you a ride."

When we reached the next town, we pulled into a McDonald's and ordered coffee and some Egg McMuffins. I needed the comfort of junk food as well as the nourishment, if that's what you want to call it. We did some dashboard dining. One of them drove and ate at the same time. I munched with such eagerness that I bit my own index finger!

The countryside was lush and beautiful. We passed a kind of geological bowl, a spring-fed body that supplied the town with drinking water for many years. Water birds rested on the placid surface. As we rode along the accumulating cloud cover generated an artificial twilight, and the smell of gathering rain infused the air.

They let me sleep in the back of the cab only to awaken with a start. One of them was crawling all over me. "Let me out! Let me out right now!" Panic overtook me and I started to hyperventilate. The driver pulled over and let me out.

It was dark and I was in the middle of nowhere. I slept in a ditch, but it felt like a grave. It wouldn't have surprised me if someone started shoveling dirt on top of me. It briefly occurred to me that I might be better off if they did. I was that depressed. In the morning, I walked into the little town and found a small drugstore. Two old guys ran it. They befriended me, and one said I could stay at his house, but there was a catch to that. Disgusted, I left.

I found a Salvation Army home and called a guy I used to live with who was now living in Minnesota. "I need a place to stay. Get me out of here, please!" I had never felt so alone as I did at that moment. He told me to come to Minnesota. I grabbed a bus and went up there for the summer, but I ended up staying for about a year. I was lost and anchored to nothing in this world.

Somewhere in the back of my mind, I remembered that one of the guys who lived in the house in Anaheim said he had a brother who was a pastor in the Seattle area. For some reason, I felt a ray of hope. I was desperate and I

Sally's Story

thought, "If I can make it up there, maybe I can get myself together."

I hitchhiked to California and headed up the coast on Highway 1. I got a ride from some people who told me about a hippie commune in Eureka, California. It was a Christian community called the Lighthouse Ranch. It sounded promising, so I decided to try it.

The scenery along the coast was breathtaking. Redwood groves grew close to the ocean. There was a rich undergrowth of fir, huckleberry and evergreen bushes, sword fern, and an abundance of greenery. Evenings offered spectacularly clear skies, perfect for stargazing.

When I arrived, I thought, "Finally! Now I can stay put and get stabilized." But I no sooner got there than things started to fall apart. The leadership changed, and the commune was going to be taken over by a pastor from town. People were unhappy about the change. I was at my wit's end when someone took me to meet Preacher Bill. Three or four of us went to his house one night. We met the whole family, his wife, Joyce, and their three children. All of them were very excited to

meet us. They were warm and loving people. The close-
ness and shared love of that family descended on me like a
warm feather comforter. It was something I had always
longed for, but never had in my life.

Bill had left his church. He was drawn to the hippies for ministry. Deep within the redwoods, he held Bible
studies and camps. I was getting to know a real family, a
Christian family, and they had a way of making me feel I
was a part of it.

The rug was pulled out from beneath me when Bill
and his family decided to move from Eureka to Curtin, Oregon. "Oh, my gosh! Where do I go now?" Bill and Joyce
asked me if I wanted to come along and help them move.
In a daze, I pitched in. We threw everything onto a couple
of trucks and I rode in one of them. We moved them into a
shack by a creek. I hadn't done drugs for a while, but I was
still really spaced out. I was drained mentally and emotion-
ally.

We stayed the night and were getting ready to leave
the next morning.

"C'mon, guys," Bill's voice soothed. "Let's circle
up and pray." I was in a deep depression. I didn't know

where I was going, and the after-effects of using drugs just added to my overall feeling of helplessness. Bill laid his hands on me and prayed. He asked the Lord to remove my depression. It left me instantly! There was no way I could process this. This was beyond anything I had ever seen in my life. *Have compassion on me, Lord, for I am weak. Heal me, Lord, for my body is in agony (Psalm 6:2).*

He said, "Sally, if you need a place to stay, bring your sleeping bag and put it on the floor."

"Oh, wow! I might do that!"

I brought a friend back with me. I did this for a winter, thinking it would be temporary, but I ended up becoming part of their family.

Bill and his family lived on hardly anything. He worked as a janitor. We had a bunch of goats to milk, some farm animals, geese, chickens, and a huge garden to live on. We all had to work. We had chores to do instead of getting stoned. It was very therapeutic. There was a constant stream of people coming to the farm, hippies and hitchhikers. Bill and Joyce had a house full all the time, those of us who lived on the farm, their own family, and the stragglers who had heard about him. He would give them goat's milk for their babies. Food appeared from people in the community. It wasn't unusual for someone to just show up with a basket full of healthy food for us.

My mind and emotions were still a mess. I would wander around and try to focus on something, but I couldn't. Bill had a gift for counseling and intuition. He could talk with you, and in a short time, no matter how confused you were, he could get you to understand and help you make sense of it. We could come and go as we pleased. It was a very safe place. A place where I could come back to myself.

I took long hikes along the streams in the cool, tree-lined valley. You could replenish your spirit by simply absorbing the beautiful vistas of the redwoods. It's where I first learned to say "amen."

Bill and Joyce had over 300 "spacey" people come through their home, and they had no relief. Soon they became more widely known, and the community in the Cottage Grove area got interested in what was happening. A Board of Directors was put together to help manage the farm. There was an area where the kids could go for medical treatment. There was a social worker who helped with the counseling, a pharmacist, and a pastor. With community backing, it became a large, functioning outreach.

My future husband, Bob, came to our farm from a large commune. He had had a psychotic breakdown while doing acid. They didn't know how to deal with him there, so they brought him to Bill and Joyce. He couldn't talk. He would just sit, smoke and stare. Joyce would speak to him and read scripture to him. She was kind of scared of him because he looked a little like Charles Manson. He was very skinny and had a scraggly beard.

Bob's family was as messed up as mine. We "connected" after a while and began to date. He told me he had had an encounter with Christ. We both wanted to go to Bible school. He chose the Assemblies School in Santa Cruz and I went to the Pentecostal School in California. We dated back and forth. My depression and isolation were too much for me to handle, and after the first semester, I had to come back to the farm. I needed the farm connection. It was my family.

Bob finished up his schooling and we got married. We bought some property some distance behind Bill's farm and lived there quite awhile. Unfortunately, the farm dissolved. They needed other financial backing, and Bill and Joyce were at a point where they wanted to live off the premises. They left and Bill took a position as Alcohol and Drug Director in Madras, Oregon. We followed them over there, and both Bob and I worked as counselors at a treatment center in Madras.

When they decided to move again, we moved to the Eugene/Cottage Grove area. We bought a home and started looking for a church. We needed a second income, and I went into nursing at Sacred Heart in Eugene, while Bob finished his Masters in counseling.

We believed the Lord was calling us to move to Washougal. There weren't any jobs for us there, but we found work in nearby Vancouver. I got a job at the Kaiser Clinic, but it didn't amount to much more than taking blood pressure and getting people settled in waiting rooms. My passion was counseling. I loved to talk to people about what they were doing and why they were doing it. I decided to enter a college degree program at Eastern Baptist, finished up my BA, and went right into my Masters through George Fox. My degree was for marriage and family therapy. From then on, the Lord started opening doors for me.

My first job was in a medium security prison for women who had felony arrests for drugs and alcohol. Then I was Assistant Dean of Women for a small Bible college in Portland. Bill and Joyce were always part of our lives. We got together every Thanksgiving, and when we went to visit, we fell in love with the area where they lived. When the Lord changed my job at the college, we took the summer to look into job opportunities. I called Providence Addiction and sent them our resumes. They interviewed both of us, and hired Bob right away to work in an outpatient office at South Bend. The next week I got a call from the same man who had hired Bob. He asked if I would like to work with high school kids as a Prevention and Intervention Specialist. "Yes!" The Lord gave us both a good income and more than provided for our needs.

It amazes me to see what I was and where I was going, and to look now at what he has done to me, and through me, to others.

The turning point in my life had been when the Lord gave me a safe place to live. It was a place where I could begin to put my life back together. I want to do something similar to that for other women. A woman with no job, no money, and no skills is easily victimized. She ends up living with a man just for a roof over her head, and she does things she probably wouldn't have done otherwise. My greatest dream is to establish a   home for women in transition, and surround them with lots of Christians. A faith-based treatment center.

We met Dwayne and Janna and started attending their church in Raymond. Janna and I share the same passion, and I believe the Lord moved us up here to help establish a "mercy ministry."

Bill and Joyce were in their older years, and when Bill got sick, we moved back to be with them. Soon after the move, Bill passed away. His death left a huge void in our lives. I don't know what we would have done or where we would be if we hadn't been with them. They were our family.

After Bill's funeral we returned to our house. Sitting quietly on the couch, I allowed my mind to wander back to the days of my girlhood. It was painful, but I knew I had to do it in order to have a total healing.

My family was unsafe and unstable. My parents divorced when I was very young, and there was a parade of stepfathers and other men in and out of my life. Several of the men who came to our home molested me, but I didn't dare say anything to my mother. She was very negative, critical and demanding. I don't remember my mom ever hugging me or telling me that she loved me. Since I was the oldest of her three kids, I assumed a lot of her maternal responsibilities. There was never any sense of "family."

I remember walking home one night when I was in my sophomore year of school. Strolling down the sidewalk through a residential area, I could see families sitting down to dinner. The lights were on. They looked happy. Oh, how I longed to be a part of something like that. We lived in a trailer. When I got home, my mom was asleep and the trailer was dark and cold. She worked nights. The loneliness was palpable as I scraped together whatever I could find for our dinner. I left home and hit the road when I was 15 years old.

A mental picture of my mom punctuated my thoughts. It was as if she was in the room with me at that moment. Her hair was dyed a dark brown, parted on one side, with puffy bangs and clusters of artificially constructed curls pulled away from her face and secured by rhinestone combs. She had strong features: thinly arched brows and dark, smudged eyes, with pronounced streaks of weariness descending from the inner corners.

She was a heavy smoker, and I envisioned her extracting a cigarette from a pack sitting on the table. The lighter she used was one of those small, gold items and made very little sound when she flipped the cover back and thumbed the striker wheel. She held the lighter in her palm and drew deeply on her cigarette, then tilted her head toward the ceiling and blew the smoke out in a stream. Her lipstick was dark and bled into the fine, hairline crevices along her upper lip. Her jewelry was clunky: big, clip-on silver earrings and a matching bracelet.

Suddenly, the front door slammed. Bob had brought home some takeout food so I wouldn't have to cook.

Early one morning, the nutty aroma of freshly

brewed coffee wafting through the house, the phone rang. It always sounded so much louder at that time of day, and I felt uneasy as Bob answered it. I turned my attention to the bacon and eggs.

Bob entered the kitchen. "Sally?"

"What's wrong?" I turned around to face him, a spatula in my hand.

There was something about the expression on his face that started the adrenalin pumping through my veins.

He walked over to the kitchen table, pulled out a chair, and said, "You need to sit down, honey."

Turning off the stove, I laid the spatula down and slowly walked over to the chair. I sat right on the edge. "What's the matter, Bob?" My stomach had begun to churn with anxiety.

"Your mother is dying, Sally," he said softly. "They need you."

Sitting there, I tried to take it in. A sea of mixed emotions swirled within, and I felt torn between reluctance and responsibility.

He sat down beside me, took my hand in one of

his, and covered it with his other one. "I know the turmoil that's going on inside you. I know you don't want to face this, but they need you, Sally. She's dying of emphysema."

I slumped forward, put my head down on our folded hands and cried. He sat there with me for a long time, letting me get it all out.

I drove to Idaho alone. There were butterflies in my stomach as I walked up the pathway to the hospital house. Approaching her room, I hesitated, my hand resting on the doorknob. On the other side of the door, I could hear a hacking spasm full of phlegm. When it subsided I entered the room, quietly shutting the door behind me.

She was propped up in bed, two big pillows behind her frail frame. She looked haggard, pale and very ill.

Summoning all my strength, I approached her bedside. "Hello, mom. It's me. Sally."

"Doesn't a mother know her own daughter?" she snapped. This was immediately followed by another attack of uncontrollable coughing.

I didn't know what to do. I felt so helpless as I watched her body double up in pain. Then a loving feeling of compassion washed over me, and I reached out and took her hand. She lifted her gaze to mine, and there were tears in her eyes. Leaning over, I gave her the hug she had never given me. Her body responded to my touch, and I felt her relax into my embrace. Here in this depressing room of imminent death, I told my mother that I loved her. A tear slid out of the corner of each of her eyes.

I sat down on the bed and held her hand in mine, and an incredible light seemed to fill the room. Warmth and love flooded through me, and I smiled as I recognized God's presence.

Come to me, all of you who are weary and carry heavy burdens, and I will give you rest. Take my yoke upon you. Let me teach you, because I am humble and gentle, and you will find rest for your souls (Matthew 11:28-29).

CHAPTER
4

Matt's Story

All the streetlamps were on, and the roads gleamed like shiny leather from the recent rain. The houses twinkled brightly as, one by one, the lights blinked on inside.

The old, empty house was massive and dilapidated. Weeds and brush consumed the yard, most of the wooden fence was missing, and there were occasional piles of collapsed and rotting lumber. The windows were narrow and dark, and many of them had panes that gave testimony to the expertise of the neighborhood rock throwers. I went through the squeaking gate and around the corner of the house to the backdoor. A stash of weed was supposed to have been left for me in the old fireplace.

Opening the door, I stepped inside. As I closed it behind me, someone slammed against it from the outside and sent me hurtling. My backpack struck the floor and I went sprawling. I hit the floor and rolled. Jumping quickly to my feet, I went on the offensive. With my left arm I blocked a blow headed in my direction, and my right fist flew out catching him in the mouth. There was a grunt as he took the brunt of the blow and went down, tumbling backwards into a pile of trash that flew apart on impact. He tried to get up, but his legs seemed to weaken under him and he

Matt's Story

went down again. Cautiously, I walked over to where he lay and stood looking down at him, both my fists ready to take him on again. There was blood streaming from his nose. He moaned, and I prodded him with my foot. "Do you want some more, jerk?"

He lowered his head back down to the floor and turned it back and forth slowly. "No, man! This one is yours!"

Conflict was nothing new to me. My father was an alcoholic. Our home life was very chaotic. Often he would come home drunk and beat my mom. Once he threatened to cut her nose off with a steak knife. He even threatened to kill her. This is what I knew my dad to be, and yet I always wanted to be with him. I was a "dad's guy." There was a special bond between us.

When my parents split up I was about eight years old. There were four of us kids, two older brothers, a sister and me. At the time of the split, my mother asked us if we wanted to stay with her or go with my dad. So I chose to stay with him.

My uncle came to stay with us, and he and my dad started getting high. Dad took me with him lots of times to the places where he would get his drugs. Even though I was young, I knew what was going on, but my love for my father blotted out the wrong things that he did and I told myself everything was fine.

About four months after moving in with my dad, my mom called. She and I had previously discussed me moving back in with her, but I was sitting on the fence. So my mom told me, "If you don't decide to come back here with me now, you are going to have to live with him permanently." She was worried about my dad's influence on me. That scared me, so I moved back in with her.

Running upstairs to my bedroom, I hurried over to the window, drew the curtain aside and peered out, hoping to catch a glimpse of my dad as he left our house. He was slowly headed for the car. Watching him climb inside, a huge lump rose up in my throat and threatened to strangle me if I didn't release it with a cry. The tears pushed themselves out of my eyes as I watched my father drive away. One of my brothers stepped inside the doorway to my room.

"Baby!" he taunted.

"Shut up!" I yelled. Quickly wiping the tears away

with the sleeve of my shirt, I determined I would never cry again. I didn't see or hear from my dad for another three years.

During this time, my mom was really lost and alone trying to support four kids with no formal education or real work experience. She had been a stay-at-home mom while with my father.

My mom ended up finding herself a boyfriend a few times, but after a couple times of trial and error, realized they weren't much different from my dad. My siblings and I even had to try and help defend my mom and ourselves.

When my mom remarried, I acquired a stepfather. He lived and worked in Aberdeen, so we had to move.

"I don't want to go!"

"Matt, I have told you before. John has a nice house for us up there. You'll like it."

"I like it here. All my friends are here."

"Give it time, Matt. You'll learn to like it there, and you'll make new friends."

"Yeah, right! You're just ruining my life, that's all!" I ran out into the backyard, slamming the door after me as hard as I could. She was a great mom, but my heart was full of anger and resentment toward her.

My start at the new school was less than friendly. I was the new kid on the block. Twenty or more of the guys would gang up on me after school. It was a rough neighborhood. Whenever I would run into one of them and he was by himself, he would leave me alone, but get him in a group and it got ugly.

The day that I beat one of them up after school was a turning point for me. From then on, I decided I was going to fight for respect and no one will beat me. They began to respect me and befriend me, and then they wanted to hang out with me. For the next couple of years, I was the "ring leader" for the gang of kids who used to pick on me. The separation from my father, the abusive relationships and the instability of life had left a huge void in me. I tried to fill it with fighting, drugs, sex and running with my gang.

I missed my father very much, and often talked about him to my mom. My brothers and sister wanted to write him off and forget him. "He's no good!" But I had a strong feeling that "something" was going on with my dad. We hadn't heard from him for about three years.

Matt's Story

One day, after one of our "dad" conversations, my mom said, "Matt, don't get your hopes up. I don't want you sitting here worrying about your dad. Who knows where he is."

"No! He's out there! Actually, the reason we haven't seen him is that he probably went to get help and he doesn't want anyone to know. He's changing his life. I'm sure of it." Inside my heart, I was beginning to weaken, starting to think about giving up on him myself.

About five or six months after this, my dad called.

"Hi, Matt! How are you? This is Dad."

"Dad? Dad! Where have you been?"

"I'm in a faith-based addiction recovery program in Portland. It's called Teen Challenge. I've been here about two months now."

"Dad, that's great!" Tears welled up in my eyes as I recalled how close I had been to giving up on him. "Okay, he's getting his life together," I thought.

"I'll be finished with the program before long. Hey! I miss you guys!"

"We miss you, too! When can I see you?"

"Soon, son. Would you like to come down to visit

me?"

"Are you kidding? Yeah! Of course!"

"I'll call and let you know when you can come. I'm working hard on recovery, Matt. You understand?"

"Sure, dad!"

"You'll be hearing from me soon."

I gave the phone to one of my brothers and danced a little jig all around the kitchen.

One morning on my way to school (one of the very few times I decided to go to school), I stopped off to visit my girlfriend, Jacquelyn, at her house. It was about 6:00 a.m., and the wind had picked up. The trees seemed restless, stirring uneasily. After visiting for about 10 minutes, I left her place and continued my 8-block walk to school. About two blocks ahead of me, I saw a small man hobbling up and down the sidewalk. As I drew closer I could see he was quite elderly. With a limp, he was pacing up and down the sidewalk as if he were waiting for someone. His clothes were what I thought a "grandpa" would wear: old, pleated pants, rundown shoes, a tan and black plaid jacket, and a dark brown beret.

I continued walking, and veered a bit out of my path

to avoid running into him. As I was about to pass him, he stopped me by putting his hand on my shoulder. It startled me. My immediate reaction was to wonder, *what's going on?* In this neighborhood, no one even spoke to kids, let alone touch one of them. People were afraid of us. His gaze locked with mine, and he said, "You are greater than all the wealth in the world as long as you have Christ."

I gave him a funny look. *What should I say to that?* Pausing for a few seconds, I said the only thing I could think of. A softly spoken, "Okay." He removed his hand from my shoulder, and I turned away, continuing my walk to school. After about three or four steps I turned around. He was gone! I was stupefied! The air was heavy and the suggestion of electrical charges raised the hair on my arms. *Am I tripping out?* Slowly I turned and started walking again, but every few steps I looked back over my shoulder. I still didn't see him, so I turned around and walked back about two blocks and looked for him. I thought maybe he lived in the neighborhood and had been going to sit on his porch or something, but he wasn't anywhere. Gone! Poof! I couldn't believe what had just happened. He appeared and disappeared in a moment. I was 15 years old and very shaken up.

Only fools say in their hearts, "There is no God." *They are corrupt, and their actions are evil; no one does* *good! (Psalm 14:1).*

Later that day when I got home from school, I called my dad at Teen Challenge. "Dad! You won't believe this!" I told him what had happened. "Is there any place in the Bible where it says anything like this?"

"Sure, son. You bet there is. Let me give you a verse or two." He gave me a verse, and I promptly forgot it. My mind wasn't exactly working on all cylinders. The morning's experience was consuming me. I wanted to know what it was all about. As I was about to get off the phone, my dad told me that for the past week or so he had been praying for me, praying that God would show himself to me. This really rocked my thinking.

I called my grandpa, a devout Christian, whom I considered one of my "religious" relatives, and asked him what was going on. I felt so stupid telling him what had happened. My grandparents knew the things I was into. Grandpa believed I had had a "supernatural encounter."

Matt's Story

Slowly I hung up the phone, and sat down on the edge of my bed. "Okay. Let's get this straight. God is trying to get my attention." I shivered and rubbed at the goose bumps that were popping out on my flesh.

I was able to visit my dad occasionally while he was in the addiction recovery program. He told me what was going on in his life. "After I get out of recovery, I want to move up with you guys and buy a house. You can move in with me and we can start becoming a family, really get to know each other." I was excited about that.

Dad came up to visit one day and we all went to church with him. He was seriously devoting himself to a renewal of his Christian life and beliefs. We were at church and a guy named Charlie Sweet, a well-known preacher, was preaching. During the service, he asked some of us to come up so he could pray for us. He started talking to my brother and I. He told my brother he was going to go to Bible College and that he had been "called." What happened next blew me away. "Matt, you had a supernatural visitation not too long ago." He knew exactly what had happened to me, and about my experience with the old man. This man was able to tell me all about my life. It was the first time I cried in years. I knew I needed to change and soon.

At the time of my experience with Charlie my attendance at church was sporadic, but I knew I had to commit. God was working on my heart. We had moved to Raymond, but a lot of my life was still in Aberdeen. My heart was at the Raymond church. I was also maintaining some relationships in Aberdeen, so I was living in two worlds. It created a tug of war, and I had to decide which one I wanted.

I talked to my girlfriend about this and how we needed to do something, because I was going to be attending church every Sunday.

"Okay. That's a good idea, Matt." So she started going with me. We had been together for three years, and I knew she was only doing it to keep us together. For me it was so much more, because this was what God was doing in my heart. It wasn't long before I totally devoted my life to God and serving in the church.

My girlfriend and I had a discussion about our relationship, especially the sexual intimacy. We both agreed that the life we were living was wrong, and a sin towards

Matt's Story

God. So we talked about how we were going to go about the intimate part of our relationship. I asked her if she still even wanted to be with me, even though I didn't want that in our relationship now, but she said that she wanted to be with me regardless.

After a few more months of growing with God, I felt he was telling me that the relationship with my girlfriend was hindering what he wanted to do in my life. I felt that he couldn't do what he wanted in her, unless our relationship was out of the way.

We were taking a walk through the park one Sunday afternoon. Spying a nearby bench I said, "Jacquelyn, let's sit down for a bit. We need to talk about a few things." Butterflies tickled the inside of my stomach and a feeling of awkwardness enveloped me.

"What's wrong, Matt?"

She could tell I was anxious about something.

"You know what you mean to me, don't you?"

She took my hand in her soft hands and her eyes never left my face. "Of course, I do. I love you, Matt."

I thought my heart would break into pieces as I said, "Jacquelyn, we can't be together anymore." My gaze dropped down to my lap, where I just stared blankly. She was hurt, no doubt about it.

"Why not?" She pulled her hands away from mine and straightened her back. Her features became stiff and pale. "What have I done?"

"No! No! It's not that!" I tried to explain what I felt God was telling me. "You know how I'm changing my life, committing myself to him and the church."

I was expecting more questions, and I was surprised when she said with resignation, "Okay! Whatever! If that's what you want and if that's what you think God is telling you, then okay."

I reached over and put my arm around her, drawing her head down to my shoulder with my other hand. She was cradled softly against my chest, her tender, wet tears dampening my shirt. She was hurt, and remorse washed over me because I had caused it.

The only reason Jacquelyn was going to church was to be with me. I knew that. It wasn't something that truly came from her heart. But since I was completely changing my life, she didn't want to lose me so she followed. My heart and soul were restless for a long time, trusting that

God could fill that place. One of the hardest things I ever had to do in my life was to follow through with that.

I hung out with my Christian friends in Raymond. There weren't any in Aberdeen. We were just starting a youth ministry in Raymond, and my youth pastor took me under his wing. He gave me something to hold onto. We went to a lot of Christian events together, and he showed me you could have fun in this Christian life. There's a lot more than just going to church.

When my dad graduated from the program, we went up to be with him. He said he felt like God wanted him to stay there for an internship. I had a difficult time accepting his decision and this change in our plans. The internship took a year to complete. My father knew how disappointed I was. He was also aware of what my lifestyle had been like in the past, and was concerned about whether or not I was committed to the changes I was making in my life.

"Hey, let's have lunch together. If you're free, that is."

"I'm not all that hungry." My mood was cloudy with disappointment, and I guess I wanted to be coaxed.

"C'mon, son." He clapped a hand on my shoulder and started walking with me to the door. "There are some things I want to share with you."

We walked the two blocks to a place called The Avenue. It was pretty packed, but we found a booth at the far end of the restaurant.

"Hi, my name is Gloria. What can I get for you?" She stood by our table expectantly, a pad and pencil in her hands. The smile on her face was so forced it looked like one of those crazy "smileys" I sometimes put in my emails. Her manner was anxious, almost aggressive.

"Is there a menu?" I asked.

My dad spoke up. "The only thing worth ordering is the spicy beef and onions on focaccia bread. It's covered with Swiss cheese and jalapenos. It'll knock your socks off."

"And a coke. I'd like a coke," I said.

"Make that two," dad commented.

"Got it. I'll be back with your water." She trotted off, her pencil poked behind her ear.

Leaning in toward me over the table, my father said, "I want to tell you something. I haven't told another soul about this, Matt."

The waitress appeared with our water and we broke apart like guilty conspirators. I took a sip and waited for her to leave. "Sure. Okay. It's a secret then?"

"Let's just say it's so special that I only want you and I to know about it. It's just for you and me."

I brightened up. It soothed my feelings to know that my father wanted to share something just with me.

"You remember when you called me after you had the experience with the old man?"

"Sure. It still gives me chills whenever I think about it."

"Well, the reason I decided to give my life to God is because I had one of my own."

Gloria arrived with her tray. Placing our plates before us she snapped, "Will there be anything else?"

"No, thank you. This is fine." My dad gave her an accommodating smile.

I took a huge bite of my sandwich, savoring the juices while, at the same time, grabbing for a napkin to catch the delicious goo that dribbled from the corners of my mouth. As I chewed, he began his story.

"I went to Montana for a while, tired of dealing with the life of drugs and running from mistakes and problems. I found a cheap motel, checked myself in, turned on the TV and settled down with my bag of *goodies*. A story on the news caught my attention. The anchorman said that a John Doe had been found murdered underneath a bridge at Court and 4th Street. The police believed the murder was connected to drugs. I was pretty sure that's where my motel was, so I got up and looked out the window. Sure enough there was a bridge down the road a bit. Then I saw the street signs. I was in a motel at Court and 4th Street! Well, an idea struck me, a way to end it all. I took a wad of money and my stash of drugs, went underneath that bridge and lay down. Then I put the money and drugs on my chest, closed my eyes and waited for someone to come along and kill me.

"After awhile, I thought I heard someone walk up and stand next to me. I became aware of a shadow, and was awaiting a blow to the head or the echo of a gun so it would be all over and...

"Immediately, I went into a dreamlike state. What I saw frightened me. It was as if I was looking through a porthole, or small, round boat window and I saw you through that window. You were holding a gun to your head. Banging on the glass with both hands, I screamed, 'No! No! Don't do it!' Apparently you couldn't hear me, and I sensed you were just about to do it. A voice from out of the darkness asked me why I was so upset. 'Because I love him!' The voice said, 'That's how I feel about you!'

"Shaking myself fully awake, I noticed a greyhound bus parked out on the highway. It seemed to appear from nowhere. I took that bus and got myself to Teen Challenge in Portland. I put myself into addiction recovery."

We agreed that it was just incredible how God had worked in both of our lives.

O Lord, our Lord, the majesty of your name fills the earth! Your glory is higher than the heavens (Psalm 8:1).

He told me he was so happy I was changing my life because he had been praying for me. After awhile, the conversation shifted and we talked about some of the crazy things he did when he was young. He had been kicked out of school for fighting and never graduated. He was one of the biggest meth users in both Raymond and

Aberdeen.

As I listened to him talk, I began to realize how he had affected me even though he was gone all the time. How parallel our lives were. How much he had influenced me. It was like I had *inherited* drugs and fighting from him. Without being consciously aware of it, I started walking down the same path that he had taken.

The internship had taken a year and, when it was through, my father accepted an offer of a staff position with Teen Challenge. That meant he would be there even longer. He told me later he was pretty nervous about telling me. I visited him frequently during this time, and we spent time together talking and enjoying getting to know each other better.

My dad just recently moved to Raymond. Our church is also starting an Addiction Recovery Program. We had a special Sunday night service for the Addiction Recovery. Since my dad has been through the program and is now getting his pastoral license, he came to preach that night.

My dad asked me if I would come up on the platform and give my testimony.

"What exactly do you want, dad?"

Matt's Story

"You know, Matt. What it's like from a kid's point of view when he has a dad that is a drug user, who's never around. That kind of stuff."

That was going to be very hard for me to do. Of all the things my father and I had discussed, we had never talked about those things. They were still bottled up inside me. I hadn't told him what an effect it had had on me, or how I had felt about it. It was scary, because I was going to do that in front of the church and he would be hearing it for the first time.

When that evening arrived, I was nervous and pacing back and forth. "How am I going to do this? How will my dad handle it?" Before I knew it, I was just broken and sobbing. I couldn't hold myself together.

I was waiting in the wings, mopping up my tears when I heard my father say, "I'm going to have my son come up here. He's going to talk to you about how he felt having a father on drugs and absent from the home."

Walking out onto the platform, I noticed the church was packed. The lighting on the platform was intense, almost blinding, and beads of perspiration immediately dotted my upper lip. There was a podium set up for me at the opposite end of the platform, but instead of going over there and facing the congregation, I walked toward my father. He turned to face me. He looked a little confused, flustered, as if I had forgotten where I was supposed to be. But I knew what I was doing. I stood in front of him, and we looked at each other face to face. Man to man. I believed God led me to do it that way.

My dad's first download from me was going to be in front of the entire congregation. I felt a tremendous release inside me, and the words just started pouring out. I told my father what it did to me when he left us. How I felt not knowing why he did that. How I missed him. How often I couldn't sleep nights wondering where he was. How I felt responsible for it all somehow. Then I told him how I had walked right down his path. The same path he followed.

"You weren't there. The enemy came into our house and you weren't there to protect us. We were spiritually stripped of our protection. The enemy took advantage of us. We were helpless!"

You could have heard a pin drop in that church. Tears were streaming down both our faces. When I finished with a heaving sob, I blindly reached out for him. We em-

Matt's Story

braced and clung to each other. It was over. I was empty. We sat together on the top stair of the platform long after the last person had left the church and talked into the wee hours of the morning. In God's presence.

My dad is moving up here, buying a house, and I'm going to live with him. He will be the director of the Addiction Recovery Program at this church. It has been three years since I was saved. I never "preach" to my family. I just model the Christian life. My mom is back at church now. My stepfather has been there a few times, and we have had some great discussions. He said the changes in me are incredible, and couldn't be due to anything but God. My oldest brother really hated me. I went to him, apologized and asked his forgiveness for all that had gone on in the past. He not only forgave me, but he told my mom that he wants me to come over and talk to him again. There's no doubt in my mind that he will have an "encounter" of his own.

God orchestrates everything. It's incredible how he worked with me, my dad and my family.

A small side note to my life: There's one I want to recognize and honor for who I am today (apart from

Jesus Christ). One who comes to mind every time I think about the word "hero". My mom! I could never thank my mother enough for the things she has brought us kids through by herself. We didn't live in a Christian home, but she was the love of Christ in my life. No matter what happened, she made sure we were taken care of. She never told us just how bad things really were, but assured us that it would all be okay.

I will never understand the loneliness and pain that you felt or how you even made it. But I thank you, Mom, for never leaving us. I know you question if you did a good job of raising us, but you are what kept my heart soft enough for the love of God to get to me and change me so easily. God couldn't have given me a better gift then a mother like you!

My soul, wait silently, for my expectation is from him (Psalm 62:5).

CHAPTER

5

Kim's Story

"Hello? Kim?"

"Hello. Who's this?"

"This is Rod."

"Oh, hi!"

"I was wondering how you'd feel about some company."

"Right now?"

"Yeah. We talked about getting together to study."

"Uh...sure. Okay."

"What time should I be there?"

"Give me fifteen minutes. Let's see, that would be eight. Is that okay with you?"

"Right. Eight it is."

We both hung up. I felt a little uneasy, and I wondered if I had done the right thing. My roommate was away for the weekend, and I was alone in our dorm room. I gave a quick call to the Resident Assistant Dorm Manager.

"Hi, Dorothy. This is Kim. I've invited a guy up to my dorm room so we can study together."

"Okay. Are you asking me if it's all right?"

"Well, sort of I guess. I'm just feeling a little awkward about it."

Kim's Story

"What's his name? Maybe I know him."

"His name is Rod. Rod Campbell."

"Oh my, yes. Everyone at the university knows Rod. He's one of our top basketball stars. He's a fine young man. There's no problem with Rod."

"Thanks, Dorothy. I appreciate it. Bye."

I stood there, the phone dangling in my hand. For some reason, I still felt uneasy. I decided to call my friend, Richard. He lived in Doty, where my folks lived, and I knew both him and his wife very well. They were a wonderful Christian couple, and I spent a lot of time at their house when I was growing up. We talked for a bit, and I told him I was expecting Rod around eight. I mentioned it casually, and he didn't say very much about it. I felt I was being silly, and I tossed my concerns aside.

A few minutes before eight, I made sure the dorm room was tidy. "I think I'll set out some cookies. I'd better brew some coffee while I'm at it."

Eight o'clock came and went. Eight thirty. Nine. Nine thirty. "Well, I guess something came up," I thought. I felt more than a bit of relief. The matter had been settled for me.

I decided to get ready for bed. I shed my clothes and wrapped myself up in my soft, yellow chenille robe. I slipped my feet into puffy, oversize, yellow bunny slippers. I was tired, and the warmth and softness of the robe and slippers soothed my jangled nerves. I had been hitting the books very hard. The college had let me stay for the summer quarter to try and bring my grade point average up to 3.5 from 3.2. One of the requirements of my scholarship was that I had to maintain a 3.5 GPA.

The nutty aroma of the freshly brewed coffee was tantalizing, and I poured myself a cup. I settled in a corner of the couch with a book. "Just a few more chapters, then bed," I told myself.

I took a sip of coffee and started to put the cup back on the end table. The knock on the door startled me so much that I spilled some.

"Who is it?" I called out while I quickly tried to wipe up the mess with a tissue from my pocket.

"It's Rod," the husky, masculine voice called through the door.

"Just a minute," I answered back. I ransacked my brain. "Should I open the door? I'm not dressed! What's he doing here now?" It was 10:45!

I clutched my robe together, making sure I was completely covered up, and opened the door.

"Hi, babe." His voice was thick and full of innuendo. He stood there, hands in his pockets. His stance seemed full of arrogance, and I had a fleeting feeling that I was at a disadvantage. He pushed his way into the room.

"Rod, it's late! You're late! I don't think..."

He walked slowly toward me.

"Where are your books?" I stammered.

"Didn't bring 'em."

I turned my back to close the front door. I knew the moment I shut it I had made a big mistake. There was much more than studying on his mind.

He turned me so that we were facing each other. With determination, he lowered his lips to mine, and he kissed me. A detestable feeling was stirred up, like silt, from my very depths. I was totally repulsed and longed for a way to escape.

I tried to pull back, furious with myself for giving in to his kiss. "What a fool I am!" I thought.

He wouldn't let go.

"Where ya goin', babe?" he crooned.

"Rod, stop! Please! This isn't what I want!"

"Oh, sure it is, honey. Just you wait and see."

He was maneuvering me over to the bed.

"Stop, Rod! I mean it!"

I tried to resist him without making a big deal out of it, but he was just too strong. He went too far, and he took me with him.

When I finally was able to get him to leave, I shut the door, threw the bolt on and propped my back against it for support. I was gasping for air, trying to fight down the hysteria building up inside me.

I called the Assistant Resident Manager and cried into the phone, "I don't know what to do. He went too far!" I didn't want to use the word "rape." That was something that happened to women who walked alone in the woods at night. I couldn't admit that I hadn't been in control in my own dorm room.

The Dorm Director showed up at my door. The Resident Manager had called him.

"Kim, are you okay?" he asked, his voice filled with

concern.

"No!" I shrieked. I was freaking out.

He sized up the situation and asked, "Have you taken a shower?"

I put my hands over my ears, trying to prevent his question from penetrating my brain. I shook my head no.

"Give your dad a call," he suggested softly.

I tried calling my father, but he wasn't home. I didn't want to call my mom. I blamed her for their divorce, and I had a lot of anger toward her. I had to talk to someone who was close to me. I called Richard again and told him what had happened.

"Kim, I tried and tried to call you back. Where were you?"

"Nowhere. I was here all night. The phone didn't ring."

"I couldn't get through. It was like the line was disconnected or something. Kim, I was praying and I got this heavy feeling that something bad was going to happen. I tried to call you to tell you not to let him in."

All I could do was cry.

"Do you want me to go to your dad's house?" I

heard the alarm in his voice.

"Yeah, I guess. But I don't want him to tell mom."

When I hung up, the Dorm Director insisted that I go to the hospital. I fought with him about it for several minutes. Right after he called the police, my dad called. Richard had gotten in touch with him. After a few brief words with my dad, the Dorm Director and I left for the hospital.

The police interviewed me at the hospital. They said they were going to talk to Rod. I told them he lived off campus, but I wasn't sure where. They told me not to worry, that they would take care of it.

One of the doctors asked me if I wanted to take the "morning after" pill. I had been raised in church, and I was against abortion. They tried to tell me it wouldn't be an abortion, that it would just start my cycle right away. I thought to myself, "If you are pregnant, it will start your period right now." To me, that was an abortion.

When I came out of the Emergency Room, my dad was sitting in the waiting room.

"Come on, Kim. Let's go."

He took me back to the dorm. "You need to get

some sleep now, Kim," my father said.

After he left I went to bed. I couldn't sleep. I thought about having to go to work the next day. But I wouldn't shut my eyes. Every time I tried, the vision of that nightmare seized my mind. I didn't want to experience it again. I was so wound up I stayed awake all night. The next day I went to work and one of the ladies could tell something was wrong. "You need to go home and get some sleep." I went home and thought about trying to take a nap. I lay down and closed my eyes. That vivid scene just shrieked at me as my brain replayed every terrifying second of it.

I decided to go to my mom's house so I could get away from the area for a while. I went to bed as soon as I got there. "No way! I can't do it!"

I was afraid to close my eyes. I told my mom about this, and she said, "You are letting your imagination run wild. You need to turn it off." It was like a slap in the face. I interpreted her comments to mean that she blamed me for what happened and that she didn't want to talk about it anymore. I never mentioned it to her again.

My dad and stepmother came to take me to dinner. We ate at a Mexican restaurant. We sat at the table, exchanged idle chitchat, and ate our meal. No one mentioned a word about what had just happened to me, and I felt very awkward trying to make small talk during the meal. When we were finished my dad went to the bar to have a drink. I was left sitting there with my stepmother.

"Why didn't you take that pill? If you have a baby, every time your father sees it he will be reminded that he wasn't there to protect you! How can you be so selfish?"

There I was, recently raped, and all she could do was berate me. I was surprised at the calm in my voice as I replied, "I will be the one who has to raise it, so if he can't handle it, that's his problem. It's not his responsibility." It was obvious to me that he was already having a hard time with it or else he would have been at the table with us.

As soon as I returned to the dorm, the Dorm Director called me into his office. He and I had become friends when I worked in the Student Affairs Office. He was very concerned.

"Kim, are you okay? I saw the doctor's report and obviously something happened because you were all bruised inside."

Kim's Story

We chatted for a while, and then I left.

Within a week, the president of the college called me into his office.

"Kim, Rod has told the police essentially the same story that you did except for one little difference." He sat behind his mahogany desk, hands clasped together and resting on the desktop as he stared at me.

I was sitting on the edge of the chair. I had felt some hostility in the room the moment I entered. "What difference?" I asked.

"He said you consented." His gaze burned into mine.

"That's a lie!" I protested.

He cleared his throat. "You have no proof. The police have indicated you don't have a case."

"I know what happened! Why would I lie about a thing like that?" I shot back at him.

"Look, Kim, this is giving the college a bad name. You have to stop calling this a rape."

It felt to me like their concern was solely for their big basketball star. As one of the big contributors on the basketball team, he brought lots of money to the college with his talent. On the other hand, they had to pay for my scholarship. I was costing them money, but Rod was bringing in the big bucks.

His gaze hardened.

I got up and walked out of his office.

When I returned to my dorm room, I slumped down on the couch and started to question myself. *Am I responsible? I let him in! But I didn't want it! Yet I didn't stop him!* I was confused and felt guilty. After a few moments of abusing myself mentally, I actually decided I had deserved what I got because I had let him in.

I tried to go on with my life. I told myself it never happened. Rod had been banned from coming to the dorms, but every night a few of his friends would come to my dorm room and bang on the door.

"Hey! Why are you lying?"

"Why are you doing this?"

I knew it wouldn't be difficult for them to break down the door, and I huddled on my bed, just cringing with fear.

I left college at the end of the summer quarter. I went back home to Doty.

Kim's Story

My mom had raised us in church. I started to lose interest in Christianity in middle school, and by high school, I had just turned my back on God altogether.

My mom was the caregiver in the family. My dad worked swing shift, so he was sleeping when we were at school and at work when we got home. When he wasn't working, he was watching TV. We had to be quiet or go elsewhere. He didn't want us around. My grandparents had raised my father in a stoic, emotionless environment, and since that was all he knew, that was how he acted toward us.

Right before my parents split up, my father started trying to be a "real dad." He took an interest in us and tried to establish the relationship of a dad. I craved the attention from him and since I always felt Mom was responsible for the divorce, I chose to go live with him. He was becoming the father we never had, and my brother and I thrived around him.

When I returned to Doty from college, I rented a little house that was on my mom's property. I really had my guard up. I didn't let anyone get close to me.

My attitude was that of an angry person, and I

would often snap at people just to keep them away. It was a defensive posture for me. I thought people didn't believe me and I wouldn't allow myself to be hurt again, so I figured I didn't need any "friends."

I started to return to the Lord. I was sneaking in the backdoor, barely aware that I was turning to him.

I used to work for a pastor and his wife by counseling at a camp in the mountains, and I started doing that again.

It was heavily wooded, a promise of shade and firewood. There was one large, clapboard building that served as the sanctuary and the dining hall. When all the chairs were folded up and put away, it was used as a snack shack. Each cabin had six girls and one counselor.

There was a young girl in my cabin at camp. She really stood out because I could tell she wanted to join us in the activities. I could tell God touched her in the chapel services, but at the last minute she would back off instead of moving forward. This went on for three nights. On the fourth night after the evening chapel service, I went up and talked to her.

"Janet, something seems to be bothering you. You

need to talk to someone. I'm going to ask you some questions and I would like some answers. Did someone hurt you?"

"Yes," she whimpered through her tears.

In my gut I knew what happened, but didn't want to broach that subject.

"Is it a friend?"

"No." She shook her head, her eyes tightly shut.

"A family member?"

She started crying so uncontrollably that she couldn't speak, but she nodded her head yes.

"Did they hit you, punch you or hurt your feelings?"

She shook her head no.

"Okay. I have another question for you. Please be honest with me. Trust me."

"Okay." She sniffed and wiped her nose on her sleeve.

"You said a family member is hurting you. Are they hurting you sexually?"

She just lost it. She started sobbing.

"Oh, my gosh," I thought. I started to freak out. I

couldn't even handle my own problem. How in the world could I help her?

I put my hand on her shoulder and said, "Will you trust me further? I am going to be honest with you. I can't handle this. I need to call the pastor over here."

She nodded.

The pastor was standing at the snack shack watching us. He could tell something was going on.

I motioned to the pastor, and he came over to me. "You need to handle this. She's been hurt!"

"What happened?" he asked, a questioning expression on his face.

"Family members have been abusing her. You need to handle this. I can't deal with it."

The pastor and his wife's bedroom was right off the sanctuary. "Both of you come in here." He was very determined.

"No! I'm out of here! I can't deal with this!"

"I said, go in there!"

"Okay." I gave in. I felt like I was going to fall apart. He didn't have a clue about what was going on with me.

Kim's Story

"We have to contact the authorities," he said.

Janet started to go ballistic.

"I want to leave," I said.

When we broke it up, the pastor said he would look into the legal stuff when the camp was over. I had to go back to work. Janet had to go home, but she was going to come back for the junior camp. She clung to me. I tried to reassure her. I told her I would be back on my day off and that I would see her then.

When I returned to camp, I found out she had gone home for the weekend and she had been abused again. She told me about it and I said, "This is *not* okay!" After the service, the pastor and the two of us sat together on the balcony of the food hall, overlooking the camp.

"Janet, you have to let the pastor take care of this. Let him do the right thing."

"If I have to go to court, I will deny everything!" She was just wild-eyed with fright.

I got very mad. I tried to hold back the words that were about to pop out of my mouth. I couldn't. "Fine! I don't ever want to hear another word out of your mouth about it. If we end up in court and you say it didn't happen, it will be our word against theirs. Why in the world should we waste our time? Don't you ever talk to me about it again."

She was stricken by my words. Before she could reply, I launched into the rest of what I had to say. "I know what happened. I've been there. I was raped! If I had to do it all over, I would turn it in to the police again."

The pastor's jaw just dropped. He had no clue. I could see he was a little uncomfortable that I got upset with her, but when I blurted that out, he just couldn't believe it.

When we were finished talking with the girl, the pastor said, "Kim! I had no idea! If I had known…"

"Why do you think I didn't want to go in that room with you? Why do you think I said I couldn't deal with it?"

"I'm so sorry."

I really don't know what happened after that. The pastor took it from there and I lost contact with her. I felt guilty about her. *For I was hungry, and you didn't feed me. I was thirsty, and you didn't give me anything to drink. I was a stranger, and you didn't invite me into your home. I was naked, and you gave me no clothing. I was sick and in*

Kim's Story

prison, and you didn't visit me (Matthew 25:42-43).

My dear friends, Pastor Dwayne and his wife, Janna, began pastoring a church in Raymond and I moved down there. For a little while, they gave me a roof over my head. I found a place with a girlfriend of mine, and I moved in with her and her family. One night she told me her boyfriend had raped her! He had put a pillow over her face when he did it. Afterward, he told her he would kill her if she told anyone. I was flabbergasted. "What is this, an epidemic?"

I was at church one night. We had a prayer ministry time. Something inside my heart urged me to go to the front of the church. The power of the feeling was more than I could resist. I went up to the front and was immediately surrounded by Christians. They started praying for me. After awhile, I decided to go sit down. I sat in the front row.

Pastor Dwayne came quietly to me and said, "You're not done yet. You need to come back up here."

I slowly, reluctantly, went back up to the altar. The other people had stopped praying for me.

Pastor Dwayne suddenly doubled over like he

had been struck by lightening. He started sobbing. I had never seen such a thing. It blew me away! I didn't understand why he was sobbing. He later told me that it felt like a knife going through him. God was allowing him to feel my pain. I couldn't believe God would do such a thing for me. My healing started. *I will thank you, Lord, with all my heart; I will tell of all the marvelous things you have done (Psalm 9:1).*

Pastor Dwayne and I talked about it later. "Kim, you didn't deal with your anger and it was destroying you."

I realized that God put two people in my path that I could have helped, but as a result of my unhealed pain, I was unable to minister to them.

I hung my head. "I didn't know how to do it. I thought crying was a weakness, that I always had to be in control of things."

"I can guarantee you, Kim, that one of these days soon you will be sobbing like a baby and you won't be able to stop." I found *that* hard to believe.

Not long after that there was a meeting of ministers. They got together and had a meeting for a week. I picked up a program of events, and I noticed that the last night

Kim's Story

there would be a discussion about emotions. "I'm not going to *that* one," I told myself. "I don't want to deal with that stuff."

When the last night rolled around I tried to distract myself from thinking about it. I had attended all the other meetings. Something kept pulling my mind back to this one, the one I was determined to pass up. A friend asked me to go with her so I gave in.

The minute we stepped inside the church I felt an urgent need to cry. We sat down. The air was heavy with some kind of presence. The tension in the church was almost palpable. I couldn't hold back my tears any longer.

A lady spoke. She gave us her testimony about all the abuse she had been through and her healing. Then we had a prayer ministry time.

I was impelled to go up to the altar. I went straight to Pastor Dwayne and Janna. They prayed for me, then Pastor Dwayne said, "Kim, tonight is the time for your healing."

"Kim, repeat after me. 'I forgive the guy who hurt me.'"

I fought it, but the urge within was too strong. I repeated the words.

"Now say 'I forgive my parents because I felt they didn't believe me.'"

Somehow, I managed to get the words out.

"Okay, here's the hardest one of all. Say 'I forgive myself.'"

"No! No! I can't say that!" I just couldn't get the words out.

Pastor Dwayne asked me two more times to say it.

I heard my voice, as if from a distance, saying, "I forgive myself, I forgive myself." I said it over and over again. A huge weight was immediately lifted from me.

When I got home, I ran to the phone and called my father.

"Dad? I want to ask you something. When I was in college, I was raped and I called you for help. I need to know something. Did you ever think I deserved it?"

"Good grief, Kim! No! I was the first one up there. Remember? How could you think such a thing?"

"Well, you never said anything about it, so I just assumed everyone thought I deserved it. I couldn't deal with it, so I didn't mention it anymore."

"Kim, I thought you were trying to forget it, so I didn't bring it up. I never thought you deserved that." As soon as I hung up, I called my mom.

I asked my mom the same thing.

"How could you think I would ever think that?" she cried. "I thought you wanted to forget about it."

"Well, mom, it was never mentioned again. I did want to forget about it, but I was also hurting. I guess I was oversensitive to your comments."

Complete healing in my relationship with my mom was progressing. A few months later, I told her how I had hated her and blamed her for the divorce. After that, we became best friends. We worked in the same office and carpooled together for six years.

Eventually, I met the man I was going to marry. We met at church. I told Pastor Dwayne, "Please don't mention 'my problem' to him."

"You have to tell him, Kim."

"Why?"

"You can't go into a marriage until you tell him."

I was afraid I would lose him if I told him. One

evening he came to my apartment and I just poured out my heart. I was sitting on the loveseat, and he was on the couch. He stared at a spot on the wall, somewhere in the dining room the whole time I talked. He never even gave me a glance. He looked very angry.

With a knot of fear in my stomach, I said, "So...what are you thinking?"

I prepared myself for the worst. I was sure I had lost him and he would not want to marry me now.

He started to cry. "I would like to get my hands on him!" he blurted out. "How could anyone hurt you like that?"

A feeling of peace filled me and a light went on in my heart. *Somebody cares!* For so long, I felt unworthy. I had forgotten that my Father in heaven cared. He always cared! He was there for me, but I never went to him.

I love you, Lord; you are my strength. The Lord is my rock, my fortress, and my savior; my God is my rock, in whom I find protection. He is my shield, the strength of my

Kim's Story

salvation, and my stronghold. I will call on the Lord, who is worthy of praise, for he saves me from my enemies (Psalm 18:1-3).

CHAPTER

6

Chris' Story

Sprawled on the living room couch, I clutched the bottle of booze close to my chest. My hands trembled so much I had to use both of them to hold it. The gaudy colors of the crocheted afghan that covered me--orange, green, red and purple--blurred together into one shrieking mass of color that hurt my eyes. An offensive odor from my bodily wastes saturated my jeans and the couch, as I lay in my own mess. How long had I been here, unable to get up? Three days? Four days?

My limbs were not only too weak for me to get up to go to the bathroom, but I had been unable to get myself any food. I had not eaten in four days. "That's okay," I thought in an alcoholic stupor. "At least I have my cigarettes and booze!"

The bottle to my lips, I tried to take a drink. My hands shook so violently the booze slobbered out of my mouth, trickled down my chin, then onto my bulky, beige sweater. "Can't waste a drop," I thought in a haze, as I tugged at my sweater, pulling it up to my mouth so I could suck the liquor out of the fabric.

Flopping back down on the couch, I grabbed at my side as a gripping pain shot through my stomach. My insides were raging! I knew I was very sick. The scream that I uttered must have sounded like the death song of some critically wounded animal. "Come and help me, somebody!" I propped myself up on one elbow. My insides started heaving, and I threw up hunks of flesh from my nose and mouth. "If there is a God, or whatever you are, you had better come down here right now and grab onto this chick because I am checking out!" Death was lurking in the room.

My brain registered a noise, and I turned my head toward the front door. My focus was blurred so I blinked, trying to clear my vision. A shadowy figure had opened my front door and was slowly walking toward me. "Chris? Good grief, girl, what's *up*?" It was Jerry; he had come to check on me.

My life of addiction started when I was a teenager. My mom was a Catholic, and my dad was an evolutionist. I didn't believe in anything. We went to church every Sunday. I was confirmed, baptized, and did my catechism until I was about 13. The church services were all in Latin, and very strict and regimented. There's no way I could get anything out of a mass when it was all in Latin, so I goofed around in the pew with my brothers and sisters. "Why do I have to go in that little box with the curtain anyway?"

My parents were dairy farmers. They worked long, hard hours milking cows, raising calves, growing gardens and living off the land. While they were busy surviving, they left me to take care of the other kids. There were five of us, and I was the oldest. I assumed a parenting role and was missing out on "normal" teenage experiences.

We had a loving family. My father was a very determined man and used my mom to get the job done, whatever it was, always pushing us to become the best we could be. While she obeyed my father, I could feel her attitude of resentment and frequently saw an expression of unhappiness on her face. Sometimes she was very demanding. I learned to be responsible and hardworking from her. Though I did every bad thing I could find to do, I was very responsible about work. While going to school, I started doing housework, then switched to work in nursing homes.

A "typical day" for me began with me getting up to go to school, coming home to study, going to work at 11:00 p.m., and getting off at 7:00 a.m. the next day. I had to get

Chris' Story

a special grant from the State of Washington because I also worked in a rehab facility. I managed to handle my drugs and booze while going to school and work. When the other kids got high, they were *high,* but even when I was stoned, I could maintain appearances.

Frustration built up inside of me so I decided to leave and hit the road. Before I was 16, I had run away from home about eight times. This time was different. I wasn't going to come back.

My thumb went out for rides. I hitchhiked to Tacoma from our home in Bothell. Along the way, I experimented with hallucinogens, marijuana and alcohol. One day a couple named Greg and Sharma picked me up. They were looking for pretty, tall, thin, young girls that needed shelter, and that's how I hooked up with a prostitution ring. They added me to their group of twenty-two other girls. We lived in a garage, and they taught us all the tricks.

After about two weeks of slide shows and movies showing us the tricks of the trade, I became disgusted with what they wanted us to do. I started looking for opportunities to get away. We were traveling in the van on our way to our first job, all of us girls in the back, and Greg made a bathroom stop for us at a 76 gas station. We were chained together at the wrist so no one could run away. Standing in line to use the bathroom, I happened to be at the end of the chain. I don't know how I did it, but I pulled and pulled at that chain, and suddenly it gave way! It must have been weak in that particular spot. I climbed up on a dumpster, jumped over a 6-foot fence and ran for my life, hitchhiking my way back home. Home didn't look so bad after all.

Most of my teen years were spent this way. I did it all. I rode boxcars. I stole cars to go joyriding. Sometimes the cars belonged to the families of my friends, but I never worried about consequences. I was out to have a good time.

My parents just wrung their hands. My mom said, "We have to move out of here and go somewhere where it is quiet and calm." My dad agreed and decided it was time for us to move. We went to the Willapa Harbor area because my dad knew about the hunting around there. With all of our stuff piled in our 1957 three-tone brown, finned Ford station wagon, we drove around looking for a farm, but we just didn't have enough money.

My dad asked us, "What do you think this town needs?"

We all yelled, "A restaurant!" We bought a small 12-seat place, picked the entire building up and swung it around so the windows faced the river. Our new family business was launched.

My first marriage was at age 19, and I had my first child when I was 20. My husband was an abusive alcoholic. We were married for a year and a half. After the divorce I came back home. The business had continued to grow, and my brothers went to Chef's School in New York. When they returned, we went into French cuisine. We got our liquor license and added a bar. That worked out good for me. Outgoing party girl that I was, people thronged to the bar. I was the social butterfly, outgoing, friendly, funny, bold and adventurous, and the booze flowed.

My second marriage brought a bit of a lifestyle change. My husband worked for the school district, and we became a very prominent couple in the neighborhood. Our house became *the* house, and all the big shots showed up to party. Attorneys, dentists, school people, everybody came. We had a full bar to offer and we regularly smoked marijuana. We partied in an "acceptable" way. Everyone drank, but no one could out drink me!

When our daughter was born, we started making some improvements to our huge home. For a while, it was hard to move around in the house. Scaffolding had been erected in the foyer, reaching to the lofty ceiling. Drop cloths lined the stairs and the wide corridor leading to the rear of the house. The interior of the house had the cool, faintly damp smell of plaster and fresh paint. All the walls were a dazzling white, the windows tall and stark, unadorned by any curtains or drapes. The echo of footsteps sounded like a little parade. Soon our house was filled with tie-dyed plant holders, bells on the doorknobs and a hot tub room, complete with marijuana plants. The aroma of Patchouli oil permeated our home.

Our marriage lasted for 11 years. The divorce was mutual. His image was "way up there," and I drank more than he did. When we would go out he would say, "Don't you embarrass me!" I just wanted to play. During that entire time, I worked, kept my house immaculate, and was al-

Chris' Story

ways there for my children. We had moved to Spokane
three years before we divorced, and I stayed there for a
while after we split up. I drank heavily the entire time I
was in Spokane. I had returned to work at a restaurant,
and I also worked the bars in two other places. Spokane
was hot! Live bands, big city stuff. Here I was, the bold
little country girl. This was right up my alley. I was a
heavy user of cocaine while I was in Spokane, but I still
managed to work and pay the rent.

I returned to the Raymond/Willapa area, and in
1986, I went into treatment at East Center Recovery in
Aberdeen. They needed a blood test done on me. All
my drinking stopped for three days, and when I took the
test I was still .35, without any booze! When I graduated from the 30-day program they wanted me to stay
and take schooling. They thought I would make a good
counselor. I shrugged the opportunity off. At the time, I
didn't have any interest in that. When I left, I stayed
clean for about two months. I learned a lot there, but I
was still searching for that elusive "something" that had
been missing all of my life.

After East Center, I really went downhill with

my drinking. I married for a third time, but this marriage of convenience was doomed from the start. It only lasted three and a half years.

My next relationship didn't require a marriage. We just partied together and saw each other nearly every day, though we lived in separate houses. Like most of the others, that relationship finally was ended after seven and a half years, destroyed by my unquenchable drinking.

By the year 1998, I didn't want to work anymore. My body started to fail. Waiting tables was out of the question. My back had been ruined from that. With seven herniated discs and a hip out, I couldn't carry the trays. I tried to get retrained, but nothing worked. All of my skills were in doing "heavy" things, like working in nursing homes, hospitals, daycares and being a waitress.

My apartment became my reclusive retreat, and I locked myself inside. Every day I was maintenance drinking. Toward the end, I needed a drink every hour and a half.

I was a self-help nut, and before I came to the Lord, I had been into all sorts of things to find answers. I was searching, frantically looking for something, but I didn't know what. There was something supernatural "out there,"

Chris' Story

I was sure.

I acquired an entire library of books on every subject looking for spiritual truth. There were books on tarot cards, palmistry, crystal balls, numerology and witchcraft, and I was always on the lookout for something new. Having something tangible in my hands made it so much easier to believe that the "answer" was somewhere among the pages. My pockets coughed up literally thousands of dollars on self-help and mystical books. But none of it helped.

"Jerry?" He came into focus. "Jerry!"

Jerry had been a friend since we first moved to Willapa Harbor. For years he had been addicted to heroin and had recently cleaned up.

He stood at the couch looking down at me. There was horror in his gaze.

As sick as I was, I wondered how in the world he got inside my apartment. I always locked the door. Always!

"How…how did you get in here?" I slurred.

"Didn't you hear me knocking?" He paused, then said, "I guess not." His heavy brows knit together with concern. "I gave the door a little push and it opened."

We talked for a few minutes, and then he left. Before long he was back with a bunch of pot and some Valium. "You need to go to the hospital, girl." An expression mixed with guilt and worry clouded his features.

All I could do was gaze up at him, my throat throbbing with a tremendous urge to cry. He was my angel. No one else had checked on me for the entire four days. I somehow felt he had been "sent." *O, Lord, hear me as I pray; pay attention to my groaning. Listen to my cry for help...(Psalm 5:1).*

I knew I should have been getting treatment. The last words Jerry said when he was getting ready to leave were, "Call me, Chris. I'll take you. Don't wait too long. You can't hold on much longer." But I didn't go. Amazingly, five days later I felt like getting up. I took a shower, walked down three flights of stairs across Highway 101 to my sister's shop, and went to work.

"How did this happen? It's a miracle!" It just blew my mind. I should have been in a hospital with IV's coming out of all my orifices for at least two weeks.

Boon Docks Seafood and Espresso shop was right

Chris' Story

on the highway. The pungent scent of the ocean filled the air. You could hear the clacking sound of oyster shells riding the conveyer belt into the cannery.

Bursting through the front door of the shop, I grabbed my apron and started tying it behind my back. My sister was startled. "Chris! Where have you been?"

Her gaze roamed over my face, and I saw the look of concern in her eyes. "You look absolutely horrible!" she stammered.

"I think I had the flu," I lied. It would blow her away to tell her I had been so alcohol sick that I couldn't breathe out of my nose, had thrown up stuff and had the shakes so bad I couldn't hold a cup! One thing I was very good at was pulling the wool over people's eyes. I had had a lot of experience with that.

A couple of weeks later my niece dropped by our espresso stand for a visit. About 18 months prior, Gina had become a Christian. She knew her Aunt Chris was "sick," and she prayed for me continuously. We talked a lot about God that night. Gina didn't let up. She talked me into going to Bible study with her. Then one Sunday in April, she brought me with her to New Life Fellowship in South Bend. Within weeks I gave my heart to the Lord, but it would be another seven months before I totally surrendered my life to him. During those seven months, I relapsed several times. I drank once a month to celebrate my sobriety. Every time I would go into the bar, I would pour myself a double shot of Stollies Vodka, throw it back and turn for the door. By the time I reached the dining room door, I would projectile vomit all the vodka so that I didn't even get the slightest buzz. God just wouldn't let me get away with it.

Every time I did that, my niece would bust me. "Aunt Chris? Have you been drinking?"

"Oh, gee! No!"

"Don't you lie to me." Her finger wagged at me like the tail on a dog.

O Lord, do not rebuke me in your anger or discipline me in your rage. Have compassion on me, Lord, for I am weak. Heal me, Lord, for my body is in agony (Psalm 6:1-2).

Ironically, it was Halloween when I humbled myself before the Lord. A power more mighty than anything I had experienced pressed down on me, and I dropped to my

Chris' Story

knees and cried, "I just can't do this anymore!" Within seconds I felt a gush of warmth flooding through me, and a feeling of quiet and peace. I believe the Lord healed me at that moment.

I will thank you, Lord, with all my heart; I will tell of all the marvelous things you have done (Psalm 9:1).

My heart felt like it would burst with zeal for the Lord! He knew me, that I was bold and adventuresome. He had a special project in mind for me. Pastor Duane had a heart for the addicts. He wanted to get together with a pastor in Connecticut, to put together a Turning Point Christian Center, a healing center, but he just couldn't get away. A little voice in my head said, "Hey, you can go! There's no reason why you can't. The only things tying you down are two goldfish. Give them to your son." I flew to Connecticut. I wanted to help Pastor Duane and our church.

I went to a Christian rehab house. Two men from the center picked me up from the airport. When I reached the wide iron gates, it was 11:30 at night and darkness enshrouded my new home. The next day, I awoke to find myself surrounded by a picket fence of pines. The recovery center was a gray stone house. When I looked out of my window, the whole of the residence swept into view, and I let out a breath. Four towering maple trees laid a blanket of multi-colored leaves on the grass, and a breeze pushed a series of cloud-shaped shadows across the yard. Someone pressed the front bell and I listened to the hollow-sounding chimes inside, clanging out two notes that sounded like a hammer on iron. I felt as though I was being asked to answer the door of my heart, to open myself to a totally new way of living.

Talk about a learning experience! I learned more about myself there than at any other time in my life. It wasn't locked down, but we were always under supervision and never allowed to go anywhere without counselors.

Before long, my recovery had progressed to the place that they asked me to become the house supervisor. Just like that! I didn't know how to run a women's home. I didn't know anything about meds or charting. The women's lives depended on me and I would go to bed saying, "Oh, Lord, this is something! I'm being stretched down here." That's when I really learned about spiritual discernment, leadership and administration. I put my trust in the Lord, and pushed my way through all the muck in the place. I was there for two and a half months, and then I brought all my newly acquired knowledge back home with me.

When I got home, I was ready to go. I'm a fast-growing Christian. I have to be on the move. Inside myself, I had a passion to help the addicts. I was ready to go, but are you ever ready for someone who is really sick and filled with demons? The strength of the Lord was with me, and that's all I needed.

Discovering that passion inside myself was a real turning point for me. I have overwhelming empathy for the hopeless and deep sorrow over what is wrecking their lives. Every time an addict stumbled into church, I could *feel* it! God has blessed me with some special character traits. I am personable, easy to get along with, compassionate and funny, but determined and tenacious. People who have been around me enjoy my company, and I usually rise to the top as a natural leader.

I became the "Pied Piper" for the addicts. "Yoo-hoo, come on out! Quit your playing!" Then I would pick them up in my car and take them to church. Pastor Duane calls me his "bulldog." Once I get a hold, I don't let go until it's finished. I have had a few things to say to the enemy during the course of my ministry: "You're a loser. You're a punk. I am going to chop you into pieces and stab you in the eye with my sword. These people are God's kids. You lose! We win! The Book says so!"

I am working with Celebrate Recovery, which is a ministry for people with hurts, hang-ups and habits. People can see the Lord is alive in me. Because I have a reputation in this community as someone who has been through a lot, I have the ability to touch many different walks of life. Sometimes I get in way over my head, and that's when the Lord says, "Just trust me!"

One day, I was cleaning in the church and I spied a piece of blue paper on the floor. As I walked forward to pick it up, it flipped over. I leaned over and picked it up. The words jumped off the page. "You do not choose me, says the Lord. I chose you and I appointed you to bear fruit. He chose you to be the light of the world to shine like the stars in the heaven. YOU ARE FAVORED."

Chris' Story

You didn't choose me. I chose you. I appointed you to go and produce fruit that will last, so that the Father will give you whatever you ask for, using my name. I command you to love each other (John 15:16-17).

CHAPTER
7

Janna's Story

"Beloved," his voice bellowed throughout the church, "remember this: Jesus took your place on the cross!" With his right arm extended, forefinger pointing dramatically at the congregation, Pastor Dunn removed a handkerchief from his pants pocket with his other hand and mopped the perspiration from his brow. It was so quiet in the church you could have heard a pin drop. He paused to let the message sink in, then said, "Please stand for the blessing."

He left the platform to make his way to the front of the church. Glancing at his watch, he knew he was going to have to hurry. He had been asked to work tonight for Moss Davis, and they needed to get home as soon as possible so he could change his clothes and get to the mine.

After making as gracious a departure as possible, Ollie hurried his wife into the car and sped home.

"I'm never going to get used to you working in that mine," Julia said.

He reached over and patted her hand.

"You're even afraid of mice," she said with a little smile.

He looked over at her and grinned. "Think you're

pretty funny, huh?"

Ollie reached over and took her tiny hand in his big, strong one. "C'mon, honey. Remember? I watch the rats. They're as big as German Shepherds! If they start heading for the surface, it's time for us men to high-tail it out of there."

She turned her head to look out the car window. She was afraid. She was always afraid. Ollie was the lead of a four-man team and a roof bolter. He was a man who worked in darkness under dangerous conditions. She hated to see his black face and dirty clothes when he came home. She thought about all the coal dust that he breathed. It was a daily reminder for her to pray that God would protect him and not let anything bad happen to him in the mine.

After a quick change of clothes he called out, "Where's my girl? Linda? Come give daddy a kiss. I have to go to work."

His little daughter ran into his arms and he swung her up in the air like he always did before going to work. She giggled and wrapped her arms around his neck.

"Why are you going to the mine at night, daddy?"

"Well, a friend of mine got sick and I'm going to work for him tonight." He mussed her curls with his hand, kissed her on the tip of her nose, and put her down.

He kissed his wife. "I'll see you guys in the morning."

He was out the door and gone. Gone into the night. Gone into the darkness.

As he neared the mine, Ollie pulled onto a secondary lane of gravel over cracked asphalt that followed the contours of a low-lying hill. Directly ahead of him a locked gate barred access to the property with its "No Trespassing" signs. Because he was a lead, Ollie had a key. He turned it in the lock and pushed the sagging gate aside. After he pulled through he had to get out and lock the gate after him. The pickup lurched and banged as he drove up the deeply rutted gravel road. He parked on a gravel berm and got out. The other three men were already in the mine, just inside the entrance.

"Hey, Larry!" he said while clapping him on the shoulder. "I didn't know you'd be on tonight." He stuck his hand out to Jason. "Nice to see you again, man." Turning to Calvin, he said, "You must be the new kid on the block." Calvin's face flushed a bit and Ollie laughed and shook his hand.

"Let's go," Jason said, and they entered the tunnel.

About 40 minutes into their work Ollie thought he heard a muffled rumbling sound, a little bit like far-away thunder. He raised his arm and all the workers immediately stopped.

"You guys step back a bit," he said.

He went forward a few feet and then he heard the sound again. It was a little louder this time. His stomach knotted with tension. Without a moment's hesitation he said, "You guys get out of here! Now! Run!"

Larry and Jason took off. They knew better than to question Ollie.

Calvin was out to prove himself and he wanted to stay.

"Hey, Ollie, what can I...?"

There was a tremendous, ear-splitting noise, and Calvin saw Ollie with both arms above his head pressing with all his strength against the roof of the mine. His knees were buckling against the weight, and he screamed at Calvin, "Go!"

Bits and pieces of the roof started falling, and Calvin turned and ran for his life. Glancing back over his shoulder he saw a huge boulder break free from the roof. It came crashing down right on Ollie.

When they dug his body out, they found his pocket bible on him. They gave it to his wife. It was spattered all over with his blood.

Greater love hath no man than this that a man lay down his life for his friends (John 15:13).

I don't know what made me think about grandpa's story that night, but I found myself sitting in his old rocking chair in the quiet of our family room. His pocket bible was open in my lap. I was vaguely aware that I had picked it up off the small table by the chair. My mother had been to our house a couple of days ago and she must have left it there. She liked having the small bible with her. Running my fingers lightly over some of the old, brown blood spatter, a wave of tremendous heaviness and sorrow washed over me.

Dwayne entered the den, sat on the edge of the couch, leaned forward with his hands clasped between his knees and looked at me. "Honey?"

Janna's Story

Raising my head, I let out a sigh. "Dwayne, I don't know what was going on during the church service tonight but it was weird. Did you notice anything?"

"Yes," he said softly. "There was a tremendous heaviness. The whole time I was speaking I could feel it."

"Honey, I can still feel that heaviness. It's really bothering me. And another thing bothers me. Mom and I tried to phone each other throughout the day, but every time one of us would call, a customer would walk in and Mom would have to go. We never got a chance to talk. Marie was on the schedule for the convenience store tonight, but she got sick, so Mom's subbing for her and I don't want to bother her at work. But I feel kind of empty without having had a conversation with her. We hardly ever miss a day."

He got up and walked over to where I was sitting. Offering me his hand, he said, "C'mon. Let's go to bed. We've had a tough night and I'm tired. Don't worry about your mom. We would have heard by now if anything was wrong."

"You're right. I'll just go look in on the girls

again before I join you."

We walked out of the room together. Dwayne headed to our bedroom, and I quietly pushed open the door to the girls' room and peeked inside. Their faces looked so precious and innocent in the depths of sleep that a lump formed in my throat and my ears hurt when I swallowed. I gave them each a soft kiss on the cheek and tiptoed out of the room.

When I went into our bedroom Dwayne was already out like a light and snoring. I changed into my nightclothes and eased myself into bed beside him. As I descended into the restorative peace and rest of deep sleep, I glanced at the clock. It was 9:55 p.m.

Down at the convenience store the darkly clothed figure paused by the crack in the fence at the rear of the property. He thought he heard a car engine running, and he peeked through the fence. Then he heard the report of a car door slamming shut, and saw a woman walk briskly back into the store. He pushed his way through the fence, listening to the squeaking of the wood. As he walked slowly, cautiously alongside the building, he approached the parked and idling car. He noticed that the ice on the windshield

Janna's Story

was starting to melt. "Must be warming up the engine," he thought. Moving carefully past the car, he stood at the corner of the building. Lurking there in the shadows he could see the front of the store. He felt his gut contract with anticipation. He loved these nighttime adventures!

The door opened and a woman stepped halfway outside, shaking a rug. As she turned around to go back in, he sprang into action. Moving quickly, he entered the store right behind her and slammed both of his hands into the middle of her back, sending her hurtling. She sprawled, hands flying out instinctively to catch herself. He grabbed her by the hair and pulled her upright.

"Please! Don't hurt me!" she cried out in panic.

"Quiet!" he snarled.

He swung her around, locked his arms around her, pinning her arms against her body, and walked her to the back of the store. Like a hunted animal, his gaze darted this way and that looking for signs of trouble, any kind of intrusion. He was nervous. Someone could come through the door any minute.

Then he saw a door marked "Bathroom". Opening it, he shoved her inside into a narrow space between the sink and the stool. She slowly sank to the floor while he fumbled in his pocket and pulled out a gun.

"Oh, no! Oh, please!" she pleaded.

He pointed the gun at her.

She started to cry and said, "Please! Please, don't shoot me!" Her eyes were wide with horror and she moved her head as if to turn away from the gun that was aimed at her.

He fired. The bullet tore into her head, though the blood was slow to come. Her body sagged to the floor. As he turned around to flee, he spotted her purse hanging from a hook on the back of the door and grabbed it. Scrambling to get out of the place, he stopped just long enough to open the till and stuff all the bills from the drawer into his pockets.

He ran out the door and was quickly back in the shadows by the car. Opening the car door, he shut off the engine.

"I don't think she's going anywhere." Adrenalin was racing through his veins. He was energized!

The wind had started to gust in from the ocean. It was a clear, freezing cold night, and the air smelled pungent. He took a deep breath, picking up the faint taste of salt at the back of his throat and disappeared into the murky darkness of the night. The scream of a gull pierced the air.

The shrill ring of the phone beside the bed woke me instantly, and my heart hammered at my ribs as Dwayne clumsily reached out to answer it. He dropped the receiver on the floor, and in what looked like one fluid motion he got out of bed, switched on the table lamp and grabbed the receiver.

"Hello?" he spoke hurriedly into the phone.

The change on his face from sleepiness to great concern was instantaneous, and a muscle was twitching in his jaw as he said, "We'll be right there."

"Who was it?" I asked, now sitting up in bed, fully awake. There was a feeling of dread in the pit of my stomach.

He looked at me, took a deep breath and said, "Janna, that was the Chief of Police. He said he needs us to come right away to Harbor Hospital."

Before he could say another word, I interrupted him. "It's my mom, isn't it?"

"Yes. They don't know if she will make it or not."

I couldn't speak. We both quickly got dressed. It was 11:00 p.m., and Dwayne's mom volunteered to come over and watch the girls. As we pulled up close to the Emergency Room we saw police officers standing beside their car. The scene seemed surreal. We parked and walked over to them.

"Are you Janna Deskins?"

"Yes, I am."

"We're sorry to tell you that your mother has passed away."

My body recoiled in shock and grief. I lost contact with the world instantly. I didn't know what was going on, what they were saying, nothing. All I was aware of was an incredible pain, like someone had just thrust a knife into my belly. It kicked in. Great, heaving sobs poured from the depths of my soul.

My husband turned me by the shoulders and led me blindly toward a building. The harsh, glaring lights of the ER stabbed at my eyes, and I put both of my trembling hands over my face. One of the doctors came over to us right away.

Janna's Story

"Are you Linda's relatives?"

"Yes," Dwayne answered.

"I'm so sorry."

"Thank you," Dwayne said. "What happened?"

"We're not sure yet. It was most likely a heart attack or a massive stroke. There was a little blood. She might have fallen and hit her head on the sink. We just don't know at the moment."

Dwayne led me over to a couch. My dad was sitting there. I remember hearing his voice. He was crying and his voice was raspy as he spoke with Dwayne.

Turning my lifeless gaze toward my father, I leaned back into the safe, warm cocoon of my husband's embrace. All my senses and faculties were out of whack.

"I found her," he wailed. "I found her on the bathroom floor of the convenience store. She was dead! Oh my God, Linda is dead!"

Dwayne was somehow able to get the story out of him. Dad said he had worked all day in the woods and came home exhausted. He knew mom would be closing the convenience store around 9:00 p.m. He went to bed and fell sound asleep, but woke with a start around 10:00 p.m.

"A cold chill ran over me. I just knew something was wrong. I got out of bed, jumped into some clothes and drove to the convenience store. I ran inside the store, calling for her. 'Linda? Linda?' There was no answer. Then I remembered her car was outside and went out to check it. The car looked like it had been started because the ice on the windshield had thawed and the hood felt slightly warm to the touch. I went back into the store. Where was she? She was still here somewhere. I tore through the place. I looked in the bathroom. That's where I found her." He covered his face with his hands, laid his head back against the couch and sobbed. "I went ballistic. I was so crazy I couldn't even find a telephone in the place to call 911, so I ran out of the store and all the way to the Police Department."

When we finally dragged ourselves to our car it was very late, and yet it felt to me like time had just stood still. I felt detached from the world. I remember telling Dwayne, "It's kind of like an astronaut out in space. He leaves the spaceship attached to an umbilical cord, tethers it out, and floats further and further away. Suddenly the cord breaks and he is no longer attached. Now he is free floating, drifting off into nothingness. He's no longer attached to his 'roots.' My mother brought me into this world. She was my root, my sense of connectedness, from the day I was born. Now she's gone. The cord's been cut for a final time."

On the way home we talked more about my mother and her great desire for us to pastor our church. About two weeks before her death, God spoke to Dwayne in prayer and said, "Within 30 days you will be the pastor of this church." She would never know whether or not her dream for us came true.

"Dwayne, let's stop by the convenience store and get my mom's purse."

"Okay, honey. Sure."

When we got to the store we were met by a police officer.

"Can I help you?" the officer asked.

"I came to pick up my mom's purse."

"What purse? We didn't find any purse."

"Her purse was full of money. She had just made

her Avon collections." For some reason, I felt compelled to explain, "My mother has been selling Avon for a long time. She sold it all over the Willapa Harbor community."

I felt Dwayne's light touch at my elbow. "Let's go home, Janna. There's nothing we can do about this. Let's leave it to the police, honey."

Settling myself into the car, I was so confused. "Dwayne, what could have happened to her purse? There is something very wrong about this!"

"Yes, there is. But right now we need to concentrate on the girls. Heather and Jen will have to be told about your mom in the morning."

When we got home I was dizzy with fatigue, shock and grief. My mind was going a mile a minute and there was no way I could shut it down. We went to bed and I took a sleeping pill.

When I finally woke up Thursday morning and walked into the kitchen, both girls ran to me, sobbing, clutching my robe. I realized Dwayne had told them. He was at the kitchen sink making coffee. The nutty aroma tugged at my heart as I realized I would never again have coffee with my mom.

Janna's Story

I sat down on a kitchen chair, an arm wrapped around each of the girls. We cried together. Heather was devastated. She and my mom were very close. They were a lot alike. I tried to comfort them. We talked a bit about what death means, and I reminded the girls that grandma was now in heaven with Jesus.

Dwayne sat down with a steaming cup of coffee and put a mug in front of me. "I called my mom and asked if she could come stay with the girls."

"Are we going to school today?" Heather asked.

Dwayne reached for her, pulled her to him. "No, Heather. No school today. Would you like some breakfast?"

"I'm not hungry." She put her head on his shoulder where she continued to cry softly.

Heather had enough maturity to understand things. Jen, nine years old and two and a half years younger than Heather, wasn't able to totally understand what had happened to my mom. She couldn't quite grasp it. I think she cried mostly because Heather and the rest of us did. She said, "I'll have some cereal, dad," and wiped her eyes with the sleeve of her pajamas.

When Dwayne's mom got to our house we went to the home of my dad's sister. Uncle Jim's and Aunt Helen's home was the family gathering place. My Uncle Bill, my dad's brother, and his wife, Danielle, drove up from Woodland. My brothers, Darin and David, had come over. A lot of family gathered there that day. We shared our grief and spoke in quiet, somber voices. The heaviness of the emotion hung over all of us like a huge, dark cloud. We were all wrapped together in the cloak of despair and shock.

My brother, David, spoke up. "I don't get it! I heard they are going to do an autopsy. Why do they have to do that?"

Dwayne responded. "The doctor said it was natural causes but they haven't been able to pinpoint exactly what. It looked to him like she had some bleeding from her ear. It might have been a heart attack. She also could have fallen and hit her head on the bathroom sink."

"We are supposed to go to the mortuary tomorrow and make arrangements," I said, as I stared blankly into space.

"Honey, let me take care of that for you. Just let me know what you want. You need to get some rest."

Janna's Story

Uncle Bill spoke up. "I'll go with you, Dwayne."

"So will I. I mean, I would like to be with you, Dwayne, if it's okay," David added.

"Sure. The three of us can handle it. What do you think, sweetheart?"

"That's fine."

"Who is doing the autopsy, Dwayne?" Aunt Helen asked. "When are they doing it?"

"One of the best. Dr. Brady is supposed to be up from Portland today."

"When will they have the results? When will we know?" I asked with some apprehension. Just the thought of them doing an autopsy on mom tore at my heart.

"I don't know, honey. I guess the doctor will call."

Somehow the day passed and Friday came. I stayed at Aunt Helen's house and Uncle Bill, David and Dwayne went to the mortuary. They had a 2:00 p.m. appointment with the director, Darrel Stoller.

When Dwayne, Bill and David came home from

the mortuary, I knew something was up. My brother is a big guy, 6'5" and about 250 pounds. There was rage written all over his face and his eyes were like fiery orbs.

The family was gathered in the family room. Chips and dip were spread out on the table, and a few people were nibbling. I was sipping a Diet Pepsi. I couldn't eat a thing.

Dwayne came right over to where I was sitting and leaned down so he could speak softly into my ear. "I need to talk to you, Janna. Let's go in the other room."

He offered his hand and helped me as I rose from the sofa. He continued to hold my hand and we walked out of the room. He seemed very uptight.

We stood just outside the family room, in the hallway. Dwyane put his hands on my shoulders and gazed into my eyes. "Honey, I wish there was some way I could make this easier for you."

"What? What happened?"

"There is difficult news about your mom."

I was teetering on the edge of hysteria and I said, "How could there be *anymore difficult* news? She's dead!" I stifled a cry by shoving my fist up to my mouth.

"Janna, she was murdered."

Janna's Story

It just hung there in the air. Murdered! The word had a tremendous impact on me. Murder was something you read about in the newspapers. Murder didn't happen to your mother!

A flood of words poured out of Dwayne's mouth. It was like he had gotten *that* word out and felt compelled to drown it by the gush of all the other words to follow.

"She was shot in the back of the head with a .22 caliber gun. It wasn't noticed right away because she has, well, you know, she had such thick hair. Like yours, sweetheart.

"And there wasn't much blood at the scene. Darrel Stoller told us at the mortuary. Dr. Brady knew that when the EMTs did CPR, blood appeared. And the same thing happened in the emergency room. He said when that happens you usually suspect a hole somewhere. Somehow it was missed. Honey, I wanted to tell you before the whole family found out."

I stood there trying to understand what he was saying. He kept talking.

"For a while there I was really worried about

David. When Stoller came into the room and told us, it was total shock. Then David went into a rage and it frightened me. I thought he might lose control of himself, so I prayed and asked God to help David hang in there. Bill dived in with some good questions that seemed to divert David. He asked if they knew how this happened, if there were any suspects, that kind of stuff. Apparently, there weren't any cameras in the convenience store, so they don't even have any tapes to look at. Actually, I was very surprised that we got this news from Darrel. He really didn't have any answers and referred us to the police."

My eyes were glazed and my body shook. Dwayne drew me to him and wrapped me in his arms. Softly, he spoke into my ear. "His strength is perfect when ours is gone." It was a reference to one of my favorite CDs that I played all the time.

A short time later, Police Chief Jerry Ashly called the house. He was a good friend of both mom and dad.

"Of course, you realize that I will now postpone my retirement, Janna. I won't rest until this thing is solved."

"God bless you, Jerry. That means a lot."

"And I think I have a suspect."

Janna's Story

I inhaled sharply and held my breath for a couple of seconds. To know who did this, to find out quickly, might help us somehow deal with this horror.

He continued. "The guy I have in mind broke into another man's house and stole all of his guns, five in total. We have already found four of them, but a .22 caliber is missing. He took them out of the safe. I'm trying to persuade him to come in for a lie detector test sometime next week."

The police seemed to know quite a bit about this man. He was a fatherless man and had spent most of his life in trouble with the law. He was suspected in another convenience store robbery and murder in Alaska.

On the Saturday after the murder we attended a scheduled board meeting at church. Near the end of the meeting, the pastor surprisingly announced his retirement. We were asked to take his place. The installation was to take place February 8. Dwayne and I just looked at each other. We were both thinking the same thing: mom's wish just came true.

We held mother's funeral the following Monday. It was at our small church on Elm. There was overflow attendance. The whole community really loved my mom, Linda. It was pouring down rain, and there were rows of people with umbrellas standing, waiting to get inside the church. The funeral service was a complete blur for me.

It was time for the healing process. We needed to get on with our lives, but I knew mine would never be the same. I was afraid. We used to keep our doors unlocked, but now I locked them all the time. I was afraid of an intruder. Sounds at night freaked me out. I was a recluse. I didn't go out. I just didn't want to be around people.

One day, Dwayne called.

"Hi, Janna, I'm on my cell. I'm almost at our front door to pick you up for lunch."

"No, I don't think so, honey. I really appreciate you thinking about me, but..."

"No buts! You need to get out, have a change of scenery. I'm pulling into the driveway right now."

I pulled the curtain at the window aside and glanced out at the driveway. There he was. Grabbing my purse and sweater, I went out the door to meet him. I slid into the passenger seat. He backed the car out of the driveway and took off.

Janna's Story

"Just lean back and relax, Janna."

As we took off for Dairy Queen a drifting fog had curled across the landscape, wispy and pale. We drove along the beach and I stared at the ocean as it came into view, watching it recede into the mist.

The parking lot was generous and Dwayne found a spot without difficulty. We walked across the lot and pushed through the glass doors. As we entered, a big woman with blond hair and a fat purse bumped into me and stopped. She just stared. My heart skipped a beat. It was obvious that she recognized me from either the newspapers or TV. She returned to the moment. "Excuse me." She continued out the door.

Dwayne took me by the hand. "Why don't you go pick out a seat for us, Janna, and I'll order. I'm having a #1. What would you like?"

Glancing at the menu board, I mumbled, "A #1 would be fine."

As inconspicuously as possible I found an empty booth, sat down and slid over next to the window, as far away from people as I could get. I didn't want to attract any attention to myself.

Dwayne came and sat down. He had napkins, plastic utensils and condiments and busied himself dividing them up between us. Following closely on his heels, the waitress appeared with her tray.

"Here we go," she said as she placed a small box with a burger and fries and a large Diet Pepsi before each of us.

I looked at the greasy food and felt my stomach turn over. Dwayne squirted ketchup in the little paper bag that contained his fries and began dunking them like little worms in the red stuff.

"How's it going, Janna?" he asked, his mouth full of a big bite of burger.

Picking up a french fry, I nibbled half-heartedly at it. "So-so, Dwayne."

I felt obligated to eat and engage in conversation, and I resented being in that position. It seemed there was some kind of spotlight on me. As I sneaked small glances around the room, some people were staring and pointing at me. I heard one say, "She's the one." The urge to get up and run out of the place was strong, but I didn't want to offend my husband. I had to try.

Janna's Story

We continued making small talk while I just picked at my food. Dwayne swallowed his last bite and asked, "Are you ready? I have to get back to work I'm afraid."

Relief washed over me. "Sure. You bet."

Once back in the car I turned toward Dwayne and said, "I'm sorry, honey. I haven't been eating much these days. But you're wonderful and I appreciate your thoughtfulness."

He glanced over at me and gave me a soft smile. "I understand, Janna. Not to worry."

After Mom's death my dad moved in with my brother. My mom had done everything for him. Without her, it was difficult for him to get back to doing everything himself. It was tough for both of us. He was hurting. I was hurting.

One day Dwayne and I were over there and he said he wanted to tell us something. We both sat down beside him on the couch.

"I meant to tell you about this before." His voice was shaky, sort of weak. "Two weeks to the day before your mom died, I had a dream. It was very vivid."

Tears squeezed out of the corners of his eyes. "Actually, I had it twice. It was so real that I thought it was really happening." He paused to wipe at the tears with the back of his hand.

"I dreamed that Linda was on a plane and the plane went down. I was running frantically through the wreckage trying to find her but I never did. Why in the world would I dream something like that?"

"I believe God was trying to prepare you for mom's death, dad. He was trying to soften the blow. The Lord does things like that to help us," Dwayne said to my father.

"It didn't work!" dad replied bitterly.

A few months later we planned a revival at the church and invited an evangelist, Daren Lindley, to speak. He preached about forgiveness. "Forgiveness is not the absence of pain and it is not the absolution of consequences. Forgiveness is when we release someone from our judgment."

After the sermon, he offered an invitation to individuals feeling the need to forgive to come to the altar. A feeling of compelling urgency swept over me. It was so strong that I went down the aisle to the altar. We were asked to pretend that the person who had hurt us was standing in front of us. Then we pretended a cord was wrapped around that person, and Daren asked us to go through the physical motions of untying that bond. As we did we had to repeat after him: "In the name of Jesus Christ this bond represents my judgment over you, and in Jesus' name I now set you free from my judgment and I throw it into the sea of God's forgetfulness." With a tremendous effort I "put a face" on my mother's killer, and pretended he was there and bound to me with that cord. I didn't want to release him. I tried to reject the idea of forgiveness. It was a terrible struggle for me. As I started to untie the bond from the killer, I felt a warm, gentle feeling start to flow throughout my entire body. *You can do this, Janna. I want you to do this.* A feeling of relief overcame me as I continued to unbind the killer. When I was finished I felt the beautiful grace of our Lord and his approval, and I actually felt serene as the weight of my burden of judgment was lifted from my spirit.

Daren told me later that when I approached the altar he saw severe pain on my face. After I "untied the cord" he said my countenance changed immediately and my face shone with peace. It was at that moment the Lord started working in my spirit. I knew God would take care of this and all that stuff was off of me.

Another amazing thing happened that night. Heather's heart was in deep pain. She was curled up in the fetal position, partway under a pew, sobbing just like the day she found out about her grandma. She was down there for about an hour. The Lord put peace in Heather and she told us later of feeling the warmth of the healing passing through her body. Also, a gift had been bestowed upon her. Heather acquired a singing voice! Prior to that night, she had not been gifted in this, but she sure has it now. God put a song in that girl's heart, and she is a totally different person.

But the people of God will sing a song of joy, like the songs at the holy festivals (Isaiah 30:29).

That experience changed my heart about everything, and people in general. My mother was a woman full of life and she was very happy. It would grieve her if I were to live a sad life, and I knew I couldn't do that to her. The girls needed me to be able to go on in a positive way as

Janna's Story

well. I received the grace to do that.

God has given us a vision to, one day, have a house for women. It will be for addiction recovery. We're going to call it "Linda's Place." We will honor Mother's memory with that.

We found out a little later that the suspect was caught. The police had enough evidence to get him convicted of the gun theft, and he spent some time in the penitentiary. When he got out, he attacked a couple on a nature trail in Grishom. He killed one of them and wounded another. The police arrived on the scene and he shot an officer. While he was in prison awaiting trial, Chief Jerry kept trying to talk to him about mom's murder. He had a lot of circumstantial information but no real evidence. One day they found him in his cell. He had hung himself.

Now, whenever I thumb through grandpa's pocket bible, I think about how he died in another man's place. Then I think about my mother, his daughter, who died in another woman's place. Then I think about Jesus, who died for us all on the cross, the ultimate sacrifice.

LIFE— stories from the harbor

Those who live in the shelter of the Most High will find rest in the shadow of the Almighty. This I declare of the Lord: He alone is my refuge, my place of safety; he is my God, and I am trusting him. For he will rescue you from every trap and protect you from the fatal plague. He will shield you with his wings. He will shelter you with his feathers. His faithful promises are your armor and protection. Do not be afraid of the terrors of the night, nor fear the dangers of the day, nor dread the plague that stalks in darkness, nor the disaster that strikes at midday (Psalm 91:1-6).

Conclusion

LIFE— stories from the harbor

I hope you have enjoyed reading the stories in this book and I pray that they have stirred you as they stirred me.

I hope you were stirred by "the more" we can experience because we were designed by God to win in this life.

Winning requires the inner working of Christ on our hearts. The miracle of Christ working in the heart of faith is, without a doubt, the most life-changing experience any individual can undergo. I have discovered that God built us to live, not isolated, but in a community where we can be encouraged, strengthened and brought together. To live in a community where our questions can be answered and where loving one another is our greatest joy.

We would love for you to visit!

Please stop by Sunday morning, we're at the South-east corner of 4th and Commercial St. Or for directions, call the church office at

(360) 942-5530

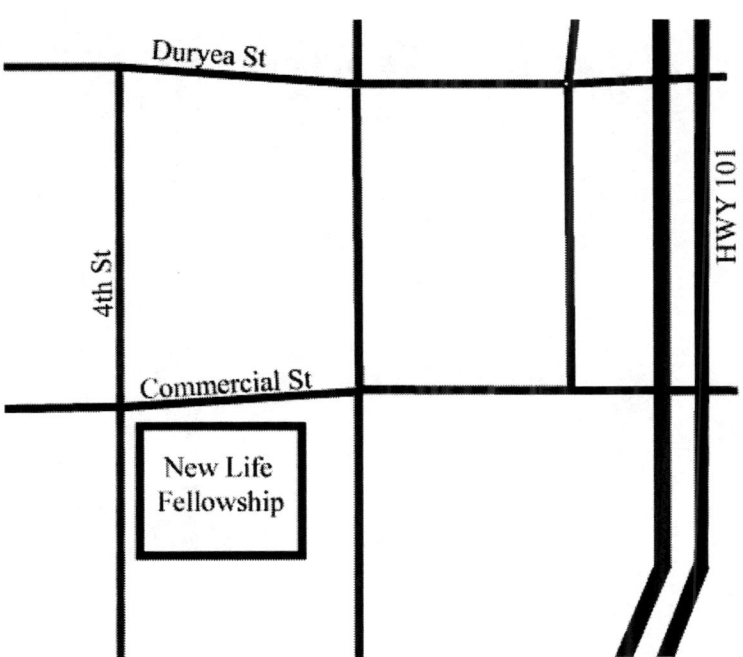

We would love to hear how this book has impacted your life! Please write us at:
newlife@nlfministries.org

For more information on reaching your city with
stories from your church, please contact
Good Catch Publishing at…
www.goodcatchpublishing.com

GOOD CATCH
PUBLISHING